T0246794

LOST GHOST STORIES OF CLEVELAND

WILLIAM G. KREJCI

Haunted America

Published by Haunted America
A Division of The History Press
Charleston, SC
www.historypress.com

Copyright © 2023 by William G. Krejci
All rights reserved

First published 2023

Manufactured in the United States

ISBN 9781467154796

Library of Congress Control Number: 2023937212

Notice: The information in this book is true and complete to the best of our knowledge. It is offered without guarantee on the part of the author or The History Press. The author and The History Press disclaim all liability in connection with the use of this book.

All rights reserved. No part of this book may be reproduced or transmitted in any form whatsoever without prior written permission from the publisher except in the case of brief quotations embodied in critical articles and reviews.

CONTENTS

CONTENTS

ACKNOWLEDGEMENTS

I would like to thank the following for their priceless contributions to this work, without which, I'm certain, it never would have come to fruition. John Rodrigue, Zoe Ames and the staff at The History Press; Tom and Emma Krejci; George and Mary Krejci; Jennifer and Burt Dobbins; Geoff Hanks; Joe Hartsel; Christina Johnson; Ryan McCarbery; Craig Whitmore; the Monroe Street Cemetery Foundation; Charles Cassady Jr.; Brian Meggitt and Mark Tidrick with the Cleveland Public Library Photograph Department; Ann Sindelar and the staff at the Western Reserve Historical Society Library; Elizabeth A. Piwkowski and the staff at the Cleveland State University Michael Schwartz Library; Maureen Pergola and the staff at the Cuyahoga County Archives; John McCown; Bookhouse Brewing; Ashley Moran and the Milan Museum; Patty Gavin Underwood; the Berea Historical Society; Tom Perotti; Bob Porter and Jim Teapole with the Beaver County Genealogy and History Center; the Library of Congress; and Wikimedia Commons.

INTRODUCTION

Sometimes it seems like all of the great local ghost stories have already been told.

In 2018, I set out to write *Ghosts and Legends of Northern Ohio* and had that concern myself. At the time, I knew what local ghostly legends I wanted to write on and how I intended to present them but had the nagging fear that I'd be repeating the same old stories that had already been shared somewhere else. It's true that a number of the stories covered in that volume had previously appeared elsewhere. Fortunately, the research I conducted when looking into those stories revealed very different tales from what had been shared by others and, generally, accepted as fact.

In truth, I don't enjoy writing on any subject unless I can add something new or, even better, stand it entirely on its head and completely change what we thought we knew on the matter. In this regard, I was more than lucky. What's more, I even managed to stumble upon the occasional ghost story that I'd never even heard of. These were, for the most part, buried in newspaper articles and books from the nineteenth century. I double-checked and triple-checked. I searched websites, newspapers from later dates and almost any relevant book that I could find. My suspicions were confirmed. These were, in fact, lost ghost stories.

As time wore on, I continued to collect even more of these forgotten hauntings from Cleveland's ghostly past. Eventually, I had enough compiled to assemble a book on the subject. After all, I don't like sharing a story that's already been told. And here are more than thirty.

There are a couple of small exceptions to this. Two of the stories that follow have been mentioned by other authors in other books, but either not in the manner in which they're covered here or not in their entirety. One of these stories tell of a specific haunting at a site in Cleveland, but the narrative abruptly ends without sharing the events that unfolded in the days that followed. Therein lies the complete terror of the tale. The other tells part of a story but without any mention of the haunting that was associated with it. In that case, also, I believe the reader will be surprised when the true facts behind the story are revealed.

Remember, also, that these hauntings occurred more than one hundred years ago. In almost every case, little or nothing remains on the site in connection to those paranormal events of yesterday. One has to wonder: is it the house that's haunted, or is it the site? Occasionally, we will take a glance back at what happened at these locations before the ghostly activity was reported. The findings may surprise you.

CHAPTER 1
THE HOUSE ON THE COMMONS

41.49244, -81.68255

That field by spirits bad and good,
By Heaven and Hell is haunted,
And every rood in the hemlock wood
I know is ground enchanted.
—*"Peter's Field" by Ralph Waldo Emerson*

This tome of terror begins, innocently enough, with a letter. The missive was addressed to the publishers of the *Cleveland Plain Dealer* and was dated February 23, 1885. The sender, who listed his place of residence as Lynchburg, Virginia, simply signed this letter as "Senex." The word is from Latin and literally means "a man of old age," but often enough was used to refer to someone as being "an aged man of wisdom," as was likely the meaning intended here.

Writing from his Virginia home, Senex reflected on the city of Cleveland and how, by the mid-1880s, it had grown into quite the affair. He recalled his life of nearly fifty years earlier when he resided in Cleveland and called the young Forest City his home. He thought on how beautifully situated that village was, being slightly elevated on the bluffs above Lake Erie. He recalled the time when Cleveland and Ohio City were two separate rival towns, connected by a single bridge. There were two newspapers, three churches and only four schools. The courthouse occupied the southwest quadrant of Public Square. No railroad entered the city, and all goods were shipped by lake, canal or wagon.

These recollections place his time in Cleveland as being somewhere between 1835 and 1845.

After reflecting on the old lighthouse, side-wheel steamers and the various sailing vessels on the lake, the author of the letter turned his attention to an area south of the city center. He recalled a small lane called Eagle Street that once extended from the entrance of Erie Street Cemetery to Pittsburgh Street, which today is Broadway Avenue. From Pittsburgh Street to the Ohio and Erie Canal in the river flats below ran a deep ravine with precipitous sides. Located south of this ravine on the heights above the flats were extensive, unenclosed fields that were referred to as the Commons.

These wild meadows were used as a free pasture for those bold enough to graze their livestock without fear of the dangerous ravine immediately to the north. More than a few cows had met their end by falling into that deep gully. Their lifeless bodies with broken necks were a regular sight at the bottom of the chasm. On one occasion, the author of the letter recalled, two young men were driving a coach, hitched to a team of horses, near the Commons. Something caused the horses to take a fright, which sent them in a dash toward the ravine. Finding themselves unable to stop the horses or change their direction, the two men jumped for their lives just as the coach and horses plunged over the escarpment. The men were spared, but the horses were killed instantly.

In all of this, the author also mentioned that the Commons were occupied by a single, untenanted brick house. The large, solitary structure, he stated, enjoyed the reputation of being haunted. Senex goes no further with any specifics regarding paranormal activity at this site. He only asserts the claim. Still, when someone testifies to a house being haunted, that location's history must be explored. A colorful and storied past just might be revealed.

For the first twenty years of Cleveland's existence, the Commons were owned by the Connecticut Land Company. Then, in 1817, the vast tract was sold to Henry Champion of Colchester, Connecticut. On July 14, 1818, Champion sold lots 1 and 2, which comprised the majority of the Commons, to Abraham "Uncle Abram" Hickox, who'd settled in Cleveland with his wife and five daughters in 1808. Hickox operated a blacksmith's shop on Superior Street and kept a sign above his business that said, "Uncle Abram Works Here," and beneath this, an image of a horseshoe was burned into the wood.

By all estimates, the House on the Commons appears to have been built by Hickox for his daughter, Dorcas, and her husband, Eleazer Waterman. Waterman was Cleveland's first jailer and later served as sheriff's deputy,

A woodcut portrait of Abraham "Uncle Abram" Hickox. *From* A History of the City of Cleveland, *1896.*

constable, justice of the peace and recorder. An unspecified accident in 1828 put him in poor health, and he died a few years later from injuries he received in that accident. He was likely buried at Erie Street Cemetery in a family plot in section 1, lot 62, though no headstones were found at that site in 1919. They were likely damaged, destroyed or sunken. His son William, who was the later owner of that lot, was buried at Woodland Cemetery.

The large, solitary brick structure that occupied the Commons was built on lot 1, situated to the southwest of Pittsburgh Street and accessible only by a small lane that would later bear the name First Street. Over the years that followed, First Street was renamed Cross Street and later became an extension of East 9th Street.

As a likely result of Waterman's accident and subsequent injuries in 1828, the House on the Commons was sold to Leonard Case Sr. on September 17, 1829. Listed as sellers with Hickox and his wife were Dorcas and Eleazer Waterman. Case, who occupied a vast residence on Superior Street near Public Square, was one of Cleveland's wealthiest and most prominent citizens. By all indications, the House on the Commons, as stated by the author of the 1885 letter, remained empty for many years. It briefly saw tenancy in 1837, when the city directory listed it as being occupied by a man named William A. Wing, a dealer in dry goods, hardware and earthenware.

William Alonzo Wing came to Cleveland from New York in 1834 at the age of twenty-five. Shortly after his arrival, he became engaged as a brickmaker, thus his specialization in earthenware, but filed for bankruptcy in 1842. He moved to Strongsville the following year, where he resided for the rest of his life. The First Street property was likely used by William Wing as a brickyard. In 1845, the house was again being rented out. The new tenant was another brickmaker, a man named Barnard Gallagan.

Little is known of William Wing or Barnard Gallagan beyond these few facts. Even so, according to the scribe who named himself Senex, the House on the Commons was already enjoying the reputation of being haunted before the arrival of these men. As the property appears to have been previously occupied by only the Waterman family, the only known death to

A depiction of the Cleveland Commons. The haunted house is the small, lone dwelling in the center of the image. *From* Birds Eye View of Cleveland, Ohio, *1877.*

The site of the House on the Commons today. *Photo by William G. Krejci.*

have occurred at that singular brick house was that of Erminea Waterman, the twelve-year-old daughter of Dorcas and Eleazer Waterman, who died on October 18, 1827.

While Senex gives no specifics about the haunting of the House on the Commons, it should be noted that other hauntings, retold in great detail, occurred in later years within the immediate vicinity of that structure. These will be addressed in later chapters. It should also be pointed out that, with the claim of this house being haunted dating to around 1840, the House on the Commons is Cleveland's first reported haunted house.

As the village of Cleveland grew into the city it is today, the Commons also saw growth. In time, more streets were laid out, neighborhoods sprang up and families put down roots. The high meadows above the flats that had once been the Commons were soon to pass into oblivion. Houses were built. Houses were torn down. Railroad yards took over the site and were later abandoned and ripped up.

Today, the Commons are occupied by a parking lot and a green space just to the south of Broadway Avenue and the Innerbelt Bridge and are bisected by a deep culvert that carries the RTA Rapid Transit line. As for the site of the old brick house itself, it's now occupied by the southern corner of a warehouse, on a derelict road, beside an unused alley and an abandoned bridge.

In truth, who can honestly say why a house is haunted or by whom? We can speculate on the reasons and let our imaginations wander, but sometimes a haunted house is just a haunted house and wants to be left at that.

CHAPTER 2

THE ERIE STREET GHOST OF 1861

41.49696, -81.68373

I am the ghost of Shadwell Stair.
Along the wharves by the water-house,
And through the cavernous slaughter-house,
I am the shadow that walks there.
—"Shadwell Stair" by Wilfred Owen

During the predawn hours of November 22, 1860, a massive white ghost was seen lurking about Cleveland's Public Square. It was said that those who initially encountered the great figure fled home in terror, jumped into their beds, hid under their covers and prayed. As word spread, curiosity seekers descended on the square but dared not approach the ghostly figure. The common belief was that the spectral presence would depart this plane at the first rays of the morning sun, but as the beams of light broke through and shone down on Public Square, the figure lingered. Cautiously, people drew closer to the ghostly being, and on inspection, the identity of the mysterious apparition was solved.

A snow had come down during the previous day, and some boys had rolled massive snowballs and stacked them one on top of another until they formed a column seven feet tall. This was done within view of the studio of William Walcutt, the sculptor who designed the famed statue of Commodore Oliver Hazard Perry that then graced the center of the square. As night descended on the city, Walcutt slipped out of his studio and onto the square with a carving knife in hand. In no time at all, he'd chiseled out the perfect form of a lady draped in white flowing robes.

The story of the phantom figure, and its creator, quickly spread through the city. As the day wore on, the snowy sculpture drew many visitors, and William Walcutt was again hailed a master at his craft, as well as a perfect prankster. An imposing figure carved from snow seems innocent enough. In reality, this was but a prelude to the ghostly horrors that were soon to come.

The following January, stories started circulating in the area of Erie Street Cemetery that the location was being haunted by a colossal ghostly white figure. The story was even mused on in an advertisement by a man named Isaac A. Isaacs, who operated a large clothing store at Union and Superior Streets. According to the earliest reports, the otherworldly being was of an enormous stature and was clad in sheets of white. Near the end of the month, the ghost was witnessed on nearby Prospect Street when a man was making his way home after a party in the company of two young women. While walking down Prospect, the trio heard an unearthly and hideous groan from behind them. They stopped and turned to see the phantom, which groaned again and extended a shadowy arm at them, the skeletal fingers beckoning them closer. Without delay, they turned and ran off, leaving the ghost far behind and vowing to avoid Prospect Street in the future.

A month and a half passed before the ghostly figure was seen again. In mid-March, it emerged on Prospect and Euclid. Unlike most ghosts, which were believed to make their presence known closer to midnight, this Cleveland ghost was also seen to noiselessly glide with its head bowed low in the early evening hours. Claims of its height varied from one witness to another. Some stated that the being stood as high as twenty-five feet tall, while most agreed that the proper height was closer to ten. Some surmised that it could elongate its spectral proportions at its own pleasure. Some even claimed that the ghost was seen to wear a hat but, in removing this, was tall enough to place it on a second-story windowsill.

A few nights later, the ghost was seen on Seneca Street, now West 3rd Street, between St. Clair and present-day Lakeside. On that occasion, it terrified a group of small children who were walking home. Among them was a little girl who resided on Ohio Street, today's Carnegie Avenue, who was so frightened by the encounter that she suffered a breakdown and afterward experienced seizures. This prompted a group of twenty-five Clevelanders to take action. On March 21, the men organized themselves into groups of two and scattered about the area in hopes of catching the ghost in the act, but to no avail. Two nights later, it was reported that the little girl on Ohio Street

The entrance to Erie Street Cemetery, circa 1870s. *Photo courtesy Western Reserve Historical Society.*

died of fits. The following night, an employee of the Ives Brewery saw the ghost on Ohio Street and chased it into Erie Street Cemetery but did not dare pursue it.

It was conjectured by the newspapers a few days later that the ghost was an escaped mental patient from the asylum in Newburgh who had a particular mania for pretending to be a ghost. On March 26, the ghost was witnessed on Roots Alley by an omnibus driver and an employee of Chittenden's livery stable. On that occasion, the ghost appeared with wide, branching horns protruding from its head.

The Erie Street Ghost quickly became something of a sensation and, subsequently, something to be joked about. The *Plain Dealer* received a letter from "The Ghost" on March 27 that poorly attempted to make some political statement. The following day, a newspaper correspondent from Brooklyn went as far as to suggest that the ghost was, in fact, the statue of Commodore Perry on the square, stretching his legs. The haunting on Erie Street was now the talk of the town.

But just like that, the ghost ceased to appear.

That October, a phantom fitting the description of the Erie Street Ghost appeared in Harrisburg, Pennsylvania. The figure, which was witnessed for several nights, was said to stand around ten feet tall and glide noiselessly through the night. On one occasion, it accosted a young man who was walking up Third Street. The man turned to see the ghost and was knocked down. He recalled nothing more until coming to. Just as was the case in Cleveland, the ghost suddenly stopped appearing in Harrisburg.

Still ill at ease, the people of Cleveland were on edge over the whole ghost business. On February 16, 1862, the ghost was believed to have returned and was blamed for an attempted break-in at the home of the Kennedy family on Lorain Street. The ghost, however, proved to be a neighbor named Thomas McClane, who owned a coffin shop next door.

Then, on November 20, 1862, the real ghost returned to Erie Street.

It first made its presence known to a young woman as she passed the cemetery gates between the evening hours of nine and ten. According to her report, the ghost stood eight feet tall, was clad in white robes and wore a peaked white hat. The massive figure noiselessly glided toward her with outstretched arms and pointing fingers. The girl screamed and ran, but the ghost pursued her to the southwest corner of the cemetery, where it halted and continued to float about.

An hour later, a young man was walking along Erie Street when he heard a noise as he passed the upper corner of the cemetery. He turned to see a

An illustration of the Erie Street Ghost. *From the* Plain Dealer, *1861.*

short figure in black robes with what appeared to be an ox's head with wide, branching horns. A blue, phosphoric light issued from its nostrils. On seeing the grotesque figure, the man turned on his heels and ran, but tripped. The dark figure charged and ran past him, then turned onto the alley that borders the north edge of the cemetery and disappeared.

Five nights later, two servant girls were walking in the vicinity of Erie Street not far from the lake. There was a particular unoccupied house in that area that was reported to be haunted. As the girls walked past the house, they looked up into one of the chamber windows and saw the ghost, all decked in white, looking down at them. Both girls were frightened out of their senses, and one of them, whose name was Sarah Gallagher, was so affected that she dropped to the ground and went into convulsions. She was carried back to the house where she was employed and remained in a low state throughout the remainder of the night.

More can be read about this haunted house on Erie Street in chapter 11, "Patrick Smith's Haunted Houses."

Just as had been the case in 1861, the ghost suddenly stopped appearing. The following March, the *Plain Dealer* ran a story claiming that the ghost had finally been captured—and by one of its own employees, no less. According to the article, a print boy was making his way home on Prospect Street after a long shift at work. At around eleven thirty that night, he observed a figure in white standing under a tree. His first thought was to run, but on giving the matter a second thought, he decided to investigate. The ghost, it turned out, was a woman in her bedclothes with a sheet wrapped about her. She claimed that she was feeling ill and had stepped out to visit her physician, who'd given her some pills.

The print boy escorted the lady home, and while approaching present-day East 21st Street, then called Granger Street, they were met by two men who were relatives of the woman. They informed the boy that she suffered from a mental illness and had wandered off. They relieved the print boy of his obligation to see her home and conducted her to their residence on Prospect.

Curiously, the woman who was encountered that night did not stand around ten feet tall, did not wear a peaked hat and did not have an ox's head, horns, a blue glow coming from her nostrils or any of the other signature tells that the previously reported ghost possessed.

The Erie Street Ghost that first made its appearance in 1861 and continued its reign of terror for nearly three winters was occasionally reflected on by Cleveland newspapers in later years. One retelling of this ghost story in 1883 claimed that the ghost was actually a medical student and the son of a prominent physician. The ghost, as was now claimed, was also an athlete, who had the ability to vault over the cemetery fence. He used his knowledge of chemistry to aid in his ghostly appearance, employing phosphorus and other chemicals to help him glow. An article from 1884 identified the print boy as William J. Gleason, who was eighteen years old

A view of Erie Street Cemetery in the 1860s. *Photo courtesy Western Reserve Historical Society.*

at the time of his encounter. It also stated that the woman he met with that night belonged to a prominent family that resided in the frame house on Prospect once occupied by Governor John Brough, though the governor's house was a brick structure. It concluded by saying that the woman was afterward remanded to the asylum.

Today, ghost stories are told in relation to Erie Street Cemetery, but these center on a man named Joc-O-Sot, a Sauk warrior who was buried there in 1844. His damaged headstone can be found in section 9. Unlike those of the Erie Street Ghost who haunted the area more than 160 years ago, tales of Joc-O-Sot haunting Erie Street Cemetery do not appear to predate the 1990s.

CHAPTER 3

HANGED MEN HAUNT THE OLD COUNTY JAIL

41.50009, -81.69555

Others may be of a different way of thinking, every one to his taste, but it has been said already, and I repeat it again, that a hanged man is good for nothing, and that punishments ought to be useful.
—The Man of Forty Crowns, *by Voltaire*

In early 1851, Cuyahoga County contracted a builder from Columbus named William Murphy to construct a new county jail near the northwest quadrant of Public Square. The initial estimate for the project was $15,600, but the final tally was closer to $30,000. The new jail was made from stone, the same that was being used to build the nearby Marine Hospital. The building was thirty-six feet wide and seventy-nine feet deep. The prison section was fifty-two feet deep and four stories high and contained forty-seven cells. The attached dwelling that fronted Rockwell Street was three stories high. The Cuyahoga County Jail was completed in September 1852.

The first hanging to occur at the Cuyahoga County Jail was that of a man named James Parks. On the night of April 13, 1853, Parks was out drinking with a friend named William Beatson in Cuyahoga Falls. It was later argued that, while crossing a bridge, Parks struck Beatson with a rock, then stabbed him in the neck. He proceeded to strip Beatson of his clothes, steal his money and decapitate him. The headless body was recovered from the Cuyahoga River the following day. Beatson's head was never found. James Parks went to the gallows for the murder on June 1, 1855.

An undated image of the Cuyahoga County Jail. *Photo courtesy Cleveland Public Library Photograph Collection.*

The scaffold that was used for executions was erected as needed in the northeast corridor of the jail. When not in use, it was dismantled and placed in storage. The hangman's gallows consisted of two upright posts of pine, united at the top by a heavy pine bar. Through the center of that bar was driven a large iron staple, to which the gallows rope was fastened. Directly below the crossbeam was the double-door trap that measured four feet, six inches wide. The platform was reached by a flight of twelve steps.

Seven men were hanged in that county jail, though the busiest year for the gallows was 1866, with two men executed less than six months apart from each other.

Dr. John W. Hughes was a well-respected man who'd received an extensive education. He came to the United States from the Isle of Man around 1860 and set up a medical practice in Warrensville Township. Between 1863 and 1864, he briefly served in the U.S. Navy, then did service as an assistant surgeon in the infantry. Resigning his position in

November 1864, he returned to Ohio and arrived in Cleveland, where his wife and child were residing.

Not long after, he was introduced to a sixteen-year-old girl named Tamzen, who was the daughter of an acquaintance named Thomas Parsons of Bedford. Dr. Hughes had been at odds with his wife over her habitual drinking and had convinced Tamzen Parsons that he and his wife were recently divorced. The two eloped to Pittsburgh, but it was soon learned that the divorce documents were forged and that Hughes and his wife were still legally married. Tamzen turned him in to the authorities, and Dr. John Hughes served five months in jail for bigamy.

After his release, he returned to his practice in Cleveland. Soon after, his wife and son sailed for the Isle of Man to visit family but had the intention of returning in a few weeks. Following their departure, Hughes turned his attention again to the obsessive pursuit of Tamzen Parsons. On one occasion, he forced himself into the Parsons home and, after being refused a private audience with Tamzen, accosted her father. Hughes was arrested and charged with housebreaking and assault and battery. Tamzen Parsons swore an affidavit and testified against him, though the case was dropped when Dr. Hughes vowed to stop pursuing the girl. Unknown to the Parsons family was the fact that Hughes purchased a firearm that afternoon.

Two weeks later, Dr. Hughes drove to Bedford with a friend and proceeded to go on a drinking bender. Again, he visited the Parsons home in hopes of talking with Tamzen, but she was out with her mother. Hughes found her in town and accosted her. When she refused to stop for him, he grabbed her by the arm, drew his revolver and fired a shot that glanced off the side of her head. He then planted the muzzle of the weapon against the back of her neck, at the base of the skull, and again pulled the trigger, killing her instantly.

Dr. John W. Hughes was tried and convicted for the murder of Tamzen Parsons and on December 30, 1865, was sentenced to be hanged by the neck until dead. That sentence was carried out on February 9, 1866. After mounting the scaffold, Dr. Hughes said a lengthy prayer and made an even lengthier speech about the evils of the death penalty. He then went on to say: "I know from my own experience that there is communication with those who have departed from this life. I am today about to suffer the extreme penalty of the law, but at the same time am sure I shall be with you after the execution as I am now."

At seven minutes past one o'clock in the afternoon, the sheriff pulled the lever, the trap opened and Dr. John W. Hughes fell into oblivion. After twenty-three minutes, the body was cut down, and the remains of Dr. Hughes were placed in a casket and taken to the receiving vault at Erie Street Cemetery.

Hughes's comments on the scaffold about being with the living after his execution seemed to set many people on edge. One person who was deeply affected by this prediction of ghostly visitation was a butcher who'd visited Hughes in jail. After the execution, the man found it difficult to sleep, claiming to be disturbed by visions of the late doctor. On the night of February 20, just eleven days after the execution, the man walked into his barn to tend to his horse and swore that he encountered Dr. Hughes standing before him, wearing exactly what he'd been attired in at the time of his death.

That same night, the inmates at the Cuyahoga County Jail were thrown into a terror when they witnessed Dr. Hughes enter the prison and walk about the corridors. Just as had been described by the butcher in his barn, Hughes was dressed in the same black suit he'd been wearing at his hanging. He was seen to occasionally rub at his neck. After wandering about for a few minutes, the ghostly doctor made his way back up to his former cell, where it's said that he sat down and began to write.

Just over a month after this report of paranormal activity at the county jail, a most heinous crime was committed a few miles southwest of Cleveland.

Alexander McConnell, a transient worker from Canada, was residing in Olmsted Township, where he took lodging in a remote cabin occupied by a couple named William and Rosa Colvin. McConnell and William Colvin were employed cutting wood for one of Colvin's neighbors. On the morning of March 24, 1866, McConnell left the cabin with William Colvin and walked toward Berea with the intention of finding more work there but said that he had a sore knee and returned alone to the cabin. He decided to rob the place and leave for Canada but was interrupted by Rosa Colvin, who'd been out that morning but returned home unexpectedly. A physical altercation ensued that ended with McConnell striking Rosa Colvin in the head with an axe, killing her almost instantly.

McConnell hid the body under a woodpile out back and quickly mopped up the blood. He then stole one hundred dollars and some clothes and made his way to Ottawa, Canada, where his wife and children resided. It was there that he was captured by authorities and extradited to Cleveland. A trial ensued, and a few days later, Alexander McConnell was found guilty and was sentenced to death by hanging.

On August 10, 1866, just after midday, McConnell was led up the scaffold and the rope was placed around his neck. He made his final statements, and the black hood was pulled down over his face. The trap was sprung, and in an instant, a horrifying situation unfolded. The knot of the noose had slipped around to the front of his neck, preventing it from breaking. For the next nine minutes, Alexander McConnell was slowly strangled to death.

Almost a month after McConnell's execution, a new inmate was placed in the cell formerly occupied by Rosa Colvin's murderer. That first night, the new inhabitant claimed to be visited by the ghost of McConnell, who tore the bedclothes from the bunk. The prisoner asked to be moved to another cell and was transferred to the one that had been occupied by the late Dr. John W. Hughes. Again, the man was visited at night by a spirit from beyond, this time the murderer of Tamzen Parsons, who emptied the mattress of every shred of straw.

Again, the inmate requested new quarters. He was then moved into the cell that once held James Parks, hanged in the jail in 1855 for the murder of William Beatson. The inmate reported that the ghost of Parks was revisiting his former cell at night, climbing into the bunk with him and pushing him onto the floor.

The fact that the cell formerly occupied by James Parks was haunted was confirmed by another man who'd recently occupied those same quarters. Martin Boyle was arrested for smuggling whiskey from Canada into Lorain and, on his arrival at the jail, was placed in Parks's former cell. On his first night, Boyle witnessed a faint light and smelled sulfur. A moment later, a pale man with a rope about his neck entered the caged room and tore away wildly at the mattress on the lower bunk, scattering the straw about the place. Boyle, who was lying on the upper bunk, sat petrified with terror. After destroying the mattress, the phantom of Parks climbed into the upper bunk and pushed Boyle to the floor. Boyle was moved out of the cell the following morning.

The other inmates of the jail likewise witnessed Parks entering that cell each night. They also swore to seeing McConnell and Hughes roaming about the place, kicking a shovel and fireplace poker down the corridors.

At that same time, another inmate of the Old County Jail, a man named William Allen, reported being a witness to the ghost of Alexander McConnell. According to Allen, he'd come into possession of one of McConnell's shirts, believed to be the one that he was wearing at the time he killed Rosa Colvin. He wore the shirt to bed one evening but was awakened when he was thrown onto the hard stone floor. He came to and realized that he was completely naked. He collected himself and lit a candle. There, by the door, he found McConnell's shirt, torn to shreds. As he crouched down to pick it up, there was a deep groan in his ear, and his candle suddenly went out. He stood in the darkness for ten minutes with the groaning continuing from the back of

James Parks and Dr. Hughes. *From the* Plain Dealer, *1855, and the* Cleveland Leader, *1866.*

his cell. Finally, a dark form passed out of his cell through the barred door, and all grew quiet again. William Allen concluded by inviting anyone who doubted his claim to come and spend a night in his cell wearing one of McConnell's shirts.

Curiously, paranormal activity in relation to Alexander McConnell and his grisly murder was not limited to the Old County Jail. In the days surrounding the execution of McConnell, the Olmsted Township cabin where Rosa Colvin was slain was reported as the scene of extensive ghostly phenomenon. Shortly after his wife's murder, William Colvin moved out, and the cabin was then occupied by a family named Miller. Unexplainable noises were heard almost nightly, as if someone were slamming doors and windows and chopping something in the back room with an axe. On one particular evening, the entire cabin shook violently, knocking almost all of its contents into disarray. Bloody handprints were said to linger on various parts of the cabin walls.

As time wore on and the population of Cleveland grew, the Cuyahoga County Jail became too small to house the number of inmates it was taking in. In 1875, the old jail was demolished, and a new 125-cell jail was built on the site. Today, the three-hundred-foot-tall 55 Public Square building stands where the Old County Jail once sat, where seven murderers met their fate at the end of a rope, and a few were said to have returned.

CHAPTER 4
THE HAUNTED UNDERTAKER'S PARLOR

41.50036, -81.69883

We have no title-deeds to house or lands;
Owners and occupants of earlier dates
From graves forgotten stretch their dusty hands,
And hold in mortmain still their old estates.
—"Haunted Houses" by Henry Wadsworth Longfellow

When we think of ghost stories, we normally think of Halloween, yet it was the Yuletide season of Christmas that was originally the more popular holiday for the telling of these tales. Families used to gather around the fire on long winter nights and keep themselves entertained with stories of the fantastic and otherworldly. Charles Dickens certainly remembered this when he penned his 1843 classic *A Christmas Carol*. With the arrival in the United States of Irish immigrants and their oral traditions during the mid-nineteenth century, All Hallows Eve soon won out as the more popular time for the telling of these spooky tales.

As Christmas 1866 approached, Cleveland was still reeling from the stories of ghostly activity at the Cuyahoga County Jail. Much to their shock, a new story surfaced only a block to the west of that institution.

It was reported on December 20 that a three-story brick building located at 72 Bank Street had become the scene of strange and inexplicable activity. At the time, the building in question was being used as a barbershop, ladies' hair salon and residence but had, until recently, been occupied by the undertaking parlor of James Howland. The activity appeared to be

Top: An advertisement for James Howland, General Undertaker. *From* Boyd's Cleveland Directory, *1863.*

Bottom: Fire consumed the former undertaker's parlor on West 6th Street on October 23, 1962. *Photo courtesy John McCown.*

centered on the room where the bodies, most known but many unknown, were laid out. It was Howland who'd supplied the coffins, and handled the funeral arrangements, for both Dr. John W. Hughes and Alexander McConnell.

William Johnson, a barber who'd recently taken up residency and set up his shop in the former mortuary, claimed not to be a believer in ghosts but said that he'd have to doubt his senses if he doubted what he was witnessing. The old viewing room seemed nightly to be alive with the spirits of the dead. It was reported that they would slam windows and doors, kick around the chairs, pound on the walls and whistle and sing.

The reports of activity caused the arrival of several mediums to investigate the matter. Most agreed that the room was literally reeking with spiritual material. On entering the room, one medium was attacked by an unseen force, which knocked him down, stomped on him, then dragged him into the street.

William Johnson stated that the noises and disturbances emanating from the former funerary room were sometimes so great that he and his family couldn't sleep. It didn't take long for Johnson to change his mind about continuing to operate and reside at that location. By the following year, his barbershop had relocated to the Union Railroad Depot and his family set up residency on Superior. Not long after, 72 Bank Street was occupied by an ink manufacturer.

In 1906, the address of this building was changed, as was the name of Bank Street, and it henceforth carried the designation 1289–1299 West 6th Street. In the early morning hours of October 23, 1962, a massive fire swept through the building, and it was razed the following year. Today, the site is occupied by a parking lot just north of 1303 West 6th Street in the Warehouse District.

CHAPTER 5
THE LAKE VIEW HOUSE

41.49026, -81.83154

On some fond breast the parting soul relies,
Some pious drops the closing eye requires;
Ev'n from the tomb the voice of Nature cries,
Ev'n in our ashes live their wonted fires.
—*"Elegy Written in a Country Churchyard" by Thomas Gray*

Nestled atop the bluffs on the east bank of the Rocky River once sat a small hotel called the Lake View House. This resort accommodation was built by the Clifton Park Association in the late 1860s. It was a two-story wooden structure with an attached open-air dining hall. The fine country establishment also boasted extensive grounds, swings, a ballroom, fine meals and refreshments.

Following its first few years of operation, the Lake View House was purchased by George Henry Dubber in the summer of 1869. For many years previously, Dubber had operated a restaurant at West and Center Streets in the Cleveland Flats. In the fall of 1872, Frederick Raff Jr. was put in charge of managing the affair. Raff came to Cleveland from Germany with his family in the mid-1860s and, like Dubber, also operated a business on Center Street, his saloon having been located across from the present-day Flat Iron Cafe.

On the morning of Tuesday, March 11, 1873, the *Cleveland Leader* reported on the death of Frederick Raff Sr., father of the Lake View House's manager, which occurred two days earlier. According to the paper, Mr. Raff had taken his own life on account of a fear of ghosts.

The article claimed that the aged Mr. Raff was suffering from failing mental capacity and had moved to the Lake View House to reside with his son's family and assist where he was able to with the hotel's operations. It was said that Frederick Raff Sr. was informed by the outgoing manager that there had been a terrible suicide in the hotel some years earlier: a man had ended his sorrows by shooting himself. This story preyed on the mind of the elderly gentleman to the point that he believed the hotel—more specifically, the room where the supposed suicide had taken place—to be haunted.

The man, it was reported, believed the ghost was moving from room to room, through walls and doors, and was opening closets and drawers. He was occasionally seen with his gun, believing that this might ward off whatever it was that haunted the hotel. Still, his family and the hotel staff really didn't think much of the matter, and while he seemed agitated, they saw no need for alarm.

Sometime between the hours of seven and eight o'clock, on the morning of Sunday, March 9, Frederick Raff Sr. was seen entering the barn by a servant girl employed at the hotel. Sometime later, she went looking for him. Entering the barn, she called out his name, but there was no answer. As her eyes adjusted to the darkness, she discovered, to her great horror, the elderly man's body stretched out on the floor. He'd apparently shot himself in the head; his pistol lay on the floor at his side.

The *Cleveland Leader* came to the conclusion that the only possible cause for the suicide was the fear of the haunting that preyed on the man. Other

The Lake View House in Clifton Park, circa 1874. *Photo courtesy Cleveland Public Library Photograph Collection.*

newspapers that reported on this unfortunate matter claimed the reason for the suicide was business troubles faced by Frederick Raff Sr.

The day after its initial story ran, the *Leader* wrote a correction, clarifying that George Dubber never made any assertion that the hotel was haunted. It further stated that the suicide resulted from some difficulty in property matters.

In regard to any previous suicide at the hotel, no evidence of this exists. In fact, the only known death to have occurred at the Lake View House was that of forty-eight-year-old Captain Louis Heckman, a former member of Cleveland City Council, who passed on August 1, 1872, following a fall.

The Lake View House was torn down in the early 1890s and was replaced by a grand mansion built by real estate investor James Albert Wigmore. That house was dismantled in 1931 and was rebuilt five years later in Gates Mills, where it carried the name Sweet Briar Farm. A modern house now stands on the site of the Lake View House.

Curiously, there was another house, about eight hundred feet south of the site of the Lake View House, that, many years after, was also rumored to be haunted. Riverbank, a three-story Swiss chalet–style home that sat at 17894 Lake Road, was built by Lyman Aaron Reed, the secretary and treasurer of the Diamond Portland Cement Company. Reed passed in 1927, followed by his wife, Minnie, in 1939. For the next fifteen years, the home was occupied by their daughter, May, and her husband, George Cherry. After the Cherrys moved to Westlake in the mid-1950s, Riverbank sat empty, and it was during that era that the house received the reputation of being haunted, though no direct reports of paranormal activity can be accounted for. Riverbank was torn down in 1963 to make way for the approach to the new Clifton Boulevard Bridge over the Rocky River.

CHAPTER 6

THE VIADUCT GHOST

41.49577, −81.70349

*Over a deep black part of the stream, not far from the church, was formerly
thrown a wooden bridge; the road that led to it, and the bridge itself, were thickly
shaded by overhanging trees, which cast a gloom about it even in the day time, but
occasioned a fearful darkness at night.*
—*"The Legend of Sleepy Hollow" by Washington Irving*

For much of the nineteenth century, crossing the Cuyahoga River was
something of a challenge. The earliest bridges were located directly
on the river and were almost constantly opened to allow the passage
of vessels. In the years following the Civil War, it was realized that a high-
level structure would better serve as a crossing. After much debate about
where it would be located, a vote to approve the construction of a new
viaduct connecting Detroit and Superior Streets ultimately passed.

Construction commenced in early 1875 and was completed just after
Christmas 1878. When finished, the span measured over three thousand
feet long and more than seventy feet high. The eastern approach was of
iron girders, while the western end was of Berea sandstone. An iron trussed
section spanning the river could pivot to allow the passage of ships that were
too tall to clear the superstructure.

Following the completion of the Superior Viaduct, there were some
who believed it to be haunted by the ghost of a man whose interests were
connected with the successful undertaking of the project. It was said that this
man, whoever he was, died before the span was finished.

The old Superior Viaduct. *From* Cleveland Illustrated, *1876.*

During the summer of 1880, reports surfaced regarding this high-level ghost. It was said that his phantom white figure appeared around midnight and silently walked the structure, back and forth, in an uneasy manner, closely inspecting the stone and iron work. After a time, he'd vanish, only to return the following night and examine another section of the bridge.

Word of the haunting spread beyond Cleveland, and the spot started to attract the attention of those living past the borders of the city. On one occasion, a man from a neighboring community visited the Superior Viaduct and inquired with the bridge's watchman if the stories of the haunting were true. The watchman replied that he'd rather not talk on the matter. This set the visitor to asking a flurry of questions regarding the strange reports. Playing along, the watchman obliged him with as many terrific tales as he could conjure. As he reached the most intense part of one such story, the watchman suddenly pointed over the visitor's shoulder, lowered his voice and quietly whispered, "There it is!"

At this, the visitor slowly turned to see in the distance a white-shrouded specter noiselessly gliding toward them. As it drew nearer, the apparition suddenly turned, walked through the railing and slowly sank from view. One theory was that this was a visit by the ghost in question. Another possibility, one that the watchman believed more likely to be true, was that it was a woman dressed in white, who lived on the flats near the viaduct, walking home.

A view of the viaduct today. *Photo by William G. Krejci.*

It's a curious thing to imagine a bridge, only two years old, as the scene of a reported haunting. It's unclear who the man said to have been connected with the bridge's success may have been. There are no reports of anyone, besides a horse belonging to a man named Albert Leyman, having died during the construction phase.

A new high-level bridge, the Veterans Memorial Bridge, also called the Detroit-Superior Bridge, replaced the Superior Viaduct in 1918. Four years later, much of the old viaduct was torn down, though the sandstone archways of the western approach are still standing. Does this phantom figure still wander the ruins of the Superior Viaduct? Only a midnight visit to the site can answer that question.

CHAPTER 7

THE GHOST ON
THE GLENVILLE ROAD

41.53696, −81.62296

On this kindly yellow day of mild low-travelling winter sun
The stirless depths of the yews
Are vague with misty blues:
Across the spacious pathways stretching spires of shadow run,
And the wind-gnawed walls of ancient brick are fired vermilion.
—"A Spellbound Palace" by Thomas Hardy

H aunted."
So boldly begins an article that appeared in the *Cleveland Leader* on Saturday, November 13, 1880. It continues with tantalizing subheadings that speak of strange manifestations about a house near Glenville, where the wrongs of a life caused a spirit to wander. Strange noises, insanity and death are also dangled before the reader's eyes.

The house in question, a frame structure with a brick outbuilding behind it, was located on the Glenville Road, beyond the Fair Grounds, and sat a good distance back from the road. The area around the house was an inviting and tranquil scene by day, but at night, when the wind howled among the tall trees, it was said to portray a dreary scene that affected the senses. The houses were fairly spread out, and this one in particular sat alone on a little eminence.

When the subject of the house was approached, neighbors who were aware of its history solemnly stated that there was something strange about the place. Many believed that the odd occurrences were connected in some way with the house's former occupant, whom the article names only as "Old Honah." As the manifestations had been noticed only since the time of the man's death, it was widely said that the man slept uneasy in his grave and wanted to right some wrong that occurred in his lifetime.

Unlike many haunted houses, the one on the Glenville Road was occupied and had been for the better part of a year. When the lady of the house was working, loud rapping was heard on the side of the building, as if someone were striking it with a cane. It would come in successions of nine, then stop momentarily before starting up again. What's more, the knocking would circle the house. At first, the new tenants dismissed the strange noises as having some natural origin, but they were unable to locate a source.

On one occasion, a girl came to assist the mistress with some chores. Shortly after the girl arrived, the lady went into town on some errand, leaving the girl alone. At this, the girl took out her sewing and sat on the front porch. It was then that she heard the sound of some person running up the side steps. The girl set down her sewing and went to investigate but could find nobody there. Returning to the front porch, she heard the noise again and searched, with the same result. Turning back to the porch, she heard someone walking near the side entrance. She imagined now that some neighbor was playing a trick on her and ran to the side entrance to catch the person in the act but, again, found herself alone. She searched the grounds and every possible hiding place near the brick outbuilding but fearfully realized that she was quite by herself. When the lady of the house returned, the girl confronted her and related what had occurred, vowing never to stay there again.

Another story claimed that a washerwoman was alone at the house, engaged at a tub in the yard, when she heard what sounded like someone banging on the windows. She also heard the sound of someone in the house tossing the furniture about and slamming the doors. Finding no one in the house, she, too, became frightened and refused to remain there alone.

On one occasion, when a fair was being held at the nearby Fair Grounds, a farmer taking care of the property was staying out in the barn when he found his sleep disturbed by the sound of someone circling the building, banging on its sides. The following morning, he expected to find footprints in the soft dirt around the barn, but he couldn't find a single track. He refused to stay in the barn another night.

One afternoon, a man living on Willson Avenue, present-day East 55th Street, came to the house to examine a cider press in the cellar that was listed as being for sale. He knocked at the door repeatedly, but his attempts

"HAUNTED."

Strange Manifestations About a House Near Glenville.

The Wrongs of a Life, it Is Said, Cause the Spirit of the Departed

To Roam 'Mid the Scenes of His Earthly Misdeeds, Making Strange Noises.

A headline declares a house near Glenville is haunted. *From the* Cleveland Leader, *1880.*

to rouse the occupants went unanswered. He thought this quite rude, as he could plainly hear them moving about inside, based on the racket that was coming from the house. Eventually, he walked over to a neighbor's to complain about the people in the house and their discourteous behavior but was informed by the neighbor that the occupants were not at home.

Having shared some of the particulars in relation to the haunting, the *Cleveland Leader* article turned its narrative to the despicable life and deeds of the man referred to as Old Honah.

It was said that Old Honah lived in the neighborhood for well over thirty years, having been about seventy at the time of his death. He'd been married many years earlier and resided in various nearby houses before building his last house, the one said to be haunted, some ten years earlier. As old age came to the couple, it was said that Old Honah's wife met with some accident and became an invalid. The husband, who'd been tired of her for many years, treated her with cruelty that made her existence a wretched one. The couple had but one child, a son named James, who, it was said, ultimately moved west with his wife and children owing to his father's eccentricities. After his departure, a hired man replaced him on the farm, and in the son's absence, the mother was ill-treated and abused by the father.

The newspaper article reported that when Old Honah's wife passed away, there was little or no ceremony. Only hours after her burial, a mystery woman arrived with a young boy and was installed as the housekeeper. When questioned by neighbors, she informed them that she'd been sent for and that she came from Rochester, New York. She told them that the old man was her uncle, but few of the neighbors believed this and insisted that the two were living together as husband and wife. One neighbor looked into her story and claimed that she actually came from Cleveland.

For the next seven years, the mysterious lady remained in the house with the old man and her son. It was rumored that she'd convinced Old Honah to sign a new will, leaving the whole of his estate to her. In time, he regretted that decision and demanded the paper back, which she refused. Neighbors claimed that the old man would go about the house in fits of rage, his cane in hand, striking at the doors, walls, windows and everything else that he happened to walk past. Three months before his death, the man started acting more strangely than ever. On one occasion, he tried to leave, saying that he was going to another city, but a farmer friend successfully coaxed him back. He was then given to wandering the house at all hours of the night, rambling on incoherently about his money, his son and other troubles and would again commence striking things with his cane. It was concluded that the man had finally lost his mind.

In time, a friend came to stay with him for a few days, and when it looked like the man was improving, the friend returned home. Old Honah died a few days later.

After the burial, the old man's son, James, came to Cleveland for the reading of the will. It was said that the mystery woman consented to give James half of the man's estate. She and her son soon rented out the house and moved away, vowing not to return.

A farm scene in Glenville. *From* Atlas of Cuyahoga County, *Ohio, 1874.*

The article concluded by stating that the current occupant was a woman of strong nerve and a disbeliever in the supernatural but, even so, was still intent on moving out. The house was being put up for sale, as surely no one who'd heard the stories would ever rent the place.

This fantastic article greatly damaged the *Cleveland Leader*'s reputation. That evening, a steady stream of complaints came in regarding the authenticity of the backstory regarding the elderly man and his family.

The following day, the *Cleveland Leader* ran another article as a correction and retraction. It stated that the article concerning the haunted house was based on a series of misstatements made to one of its reporters, which did great injustice to the memory of the deceased and to the reputation of the lady who'd come to live with him. The slanderous statements made in the paper were given by a neighbor and not the occupant of the house that was believed to be haunted. The editor personally stated that the article was published without his knowledge. Had he been made aware of it, he'd have branded the statements made against the aged man as falsehoods, as he was personally well acquainted with the deceased gentleman.

While the true identity of "Old Honah" had been withheld, it became apparent who the article was about, at least to those who knew him and lived in the vicinity of his farmhouse. The family name was kept anonymous, and after 140 years, one would think that discovering Old Honah's true identity would, at this point, be impossible. After two years of intense research on my part, however, the answer finally presented itself. One too many clues were given away by the author of the article, and the rest simply fell into place.

The haunted house in question, it was reported, was located out on the Glenville Road, beyond the Fair Grounds. Today, the Glenville Road is St. Clair Avenue. The Fair Grounds referred to here were the Northern Ohio Fair Grounds and were located on the north side of St. Clair between present-day East 88th and East 93rd Streets. According to maps from the period, the first property beyond this belonged to a man named James Houghton. Knowing that Old Honah's son's name was also James, I followed on the idea that the son might have been named for his father. Looking into this possibility revealed the rest of the story.

James Houghton was born on November 2, 1804, in Sandwich, Kent, England, to parents George and Anna Houghton. In his earliest years, he was employed as a silk merchant. On December 1, 1827, he was married at Surrey, England, to Charlotte Kedie, a daughter of William and Hannah Kedie. The following October, while the couple were residing in London, their only child, a son named James Hazel Houghton, was born. Five years later, the family sailed for the United States aboard a ship called the *Hudson* and landed in New York on August 24, 1832. They originally took up residency in Irondequoit, a suburb of Rochester, New York, but in 1837, the family made its way west and settled in a part of East Cleveland Township that would ultimately become Glenville.

Not long after settling in East Cleveland, James Houghton purchased a sizable tract of land with a man named John G. Morse and set himself to farming. Around 1845, he turned his attention to planting orchards and within ten years was cultivating 3,200 trees, including apples and mulberries, the majority being peaches. He also tended extensive grape vineyards and became a noted horticulturalist, having won many awards and special notes of recognition for his produce.

James and Charlotte's son did marry, as the story says. He and his wife, Julia, had no fewer than eight children. The story was also correct in the claim that he and his family moved west. They departed Ohio in 1863, first residing in Michigan; by 1870, they had settled in Missouri. Whether or not their moving had anything to do with James Hazel Houghton's father's eccentricities, one can only guess.

Charlotte Kedie Houghton died on April 17, 1873, one week shy of her seventy-second birthday, fitting the timeline of the haunted house's backstory perfectly. Funeral services were held a few days later at Saint Paul's Church in Collamer Village, and she was buried at Lake View Cemetery in section 2, lot 350. Apparently, the article in the *Cleveland Leader* was wrong in claiming that Charlotte Houghton was buried with little or no ceremony.

William Kedie Jr., Charlotte Houghton's younger brother, followed his sister to the United States in 1836 and settled with his family in Rochester. He and his wife had many children, one of whom was also named Charlotte. In the mid-1850s, that daughter was married to Charles Hoyt Cushman and with him had three children, all boys, though their middle son, William, died in childhood in 1867.

Charles Cushman died in November 1872. When her aunt Charlotte passed away the following April, the recently widowed Charlotte Cushman was invited to come to Ohio to help care for her aging uncle. Traveling with her was her youngest son, five-year-old Francis Livingston Cushman. Her elder son, Charles, was seventeen and remained in New York. This was the mystery woman who arrived following the death of Charlotte Houghton. As she'd stated, she really was from Rochester, and the elder James Houghton was, in fact, her uncle.

The ghost story spoke of a hired man who took over the duties of Old Honah's son when he moved west. That man was Robert Dyke, a family friend who moved to the farm. Dyke passed away at the Houghton farm on February 2, 1879, and was laid to rest in the Houghton family plot.

There is no printed account of what the final days of James Houghton's life were like concerning whether he was suffering from mental illness. The article that relayed the ghost story can hardly be counted on as a reliable source of information. In the end, all that is truly known is that James Houghton died on May 15, 1879, and was laid to rest beside his wife and friend at his family plot at Lake View Cemetery.

It turns out that the story about Old Honah changing his will and leaving everything to the mystery woman was another falsehood. On his death, Dennis Adams was appointed administrator of James Houghton's estate, and an inventory was made of his belongings. Many items were retained by James Hazel Houghton and Charlotte Cushman. The rest were sold and the proceeds divided between them. Curiously, the only items listed among James Houghton's possessions that weren't sold were, in fact, a grape crusher and a press. This could only be the previously mentioned cider press in the cellar that the man from Willson Avenue came to examine.

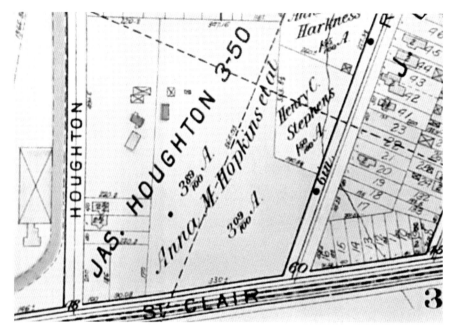

A map shows the arrangement of buildings on the Houghton farm. *From* Atlas of the Suburbs of Cleveland, Ohio, *1898.*

A month after the passing of James Houghton, the farm was sold by his son and daughter-in-law to Charlotte Cushman for the sum of one dollar. This was done in pursuance and in consideration of a contract made between the two parties the previous September. The farm was briefly rented out but was ultimately sold to Henry C. Brainard on November 2, 1881, for $2,500.

Shortly after 1900, the Houghton farm was sold to developers and the property was subdivided into smaller lots. The house that had, many years earlier, been the scene of a reported haunting was demolished around 1912. An apartment building called Irma, located on the northwest corner of East 94th Street and Wright Court, occupies the former site of James Houghton's farmhouse.

CHAPTER 8
A HAUNTED BROTHEL
41.49368, -81.68154

So, so, break off this last lamenting kiss,
Which sucks two souls, and vapours both away:
Turn thou, ghost, that way, and let me turn this,
And let ourselves benight our happiest day;
We ask none leave to love; nor will we owe
Any so cheap a death, as saying, go.
—"The Expiration" by John Donne

The year 1877 saw a horrific murder in a house of prostitution at 100 Cross Street in Cleveland. In March 1883, the *Cleveland Leader* revealed that the house was being haunted by the travel-worn spirits of the murderer and his victim, who, according to the paper, could find no rest in heaven or hell.

The house in question was a small frame structure, painted brown, that sat on the east side of Cross Street between Broadway and Woodland Avenues. Curiously, it sat just five hundred feet north of the site formerly occupied by the House on the Commons. At the time of the haunting, the Cross Street house was tenanted by Mrs. Laura B. Williams, her son Henry and her aged aunt, Mary A. Lynch. The family resided on the second floor of the house, where the murder had occurred. Not long after moving in, the ghostly noises and apparitions presented themselves.

The tragic tale of the murder, and the events leading up to it, is thus.

Charles R. McGill was born in Athens, Ohio, in 1850 to parents William and Esther Bing McGill. As he approached the age of twenty, he moved to Columbus, where he was married on June 30, 1870, to Louisa Steelman. Two children, Bertha and Edward, were born to them over the course of the next couple of years. In 1873, Charles McGill left his wife and children and, shortly after, became acquainted with a twenty-one-year-old Irish girl named Mary Kelley. He went to Toledo, found work there and enticed Mary to join him, which she did. Shortly after, they moved to Cleveland and took up residency in the Atwater Block, at the east end of the new Superior Viaduct. The two lived as husband and wife, though they were never married.

Just after Christmas 1876, Charles and Mary separated on account of the fact that neither were employed, nor could they support themselves. McGill later stated that they were starving to death and that he stayed as long as he could. He returned to Athens in hopes of securing a position and home there and planned to send for Mary. This apparently proved unsuccessful. He returned to Cleveland a few months later but couldn't locate Mary Kelley. That October, he took to heavy drinking.

On Saturday, December 1, 1877, McGill, who'd sobered up recently, succeeded in locating Mary. The two met up in a saloon on Broadway and made plans to get together again that evening at Mary's place of residence. McGill borrowed a friend's overcoat and some money and proceeded to the house on Cross Street where Mary was staying. The house, as it turned out, was a brothel operated by a woman named Laura Lane. According to those who were present, Charles and Mary had an enjoyable evening together and McGill even spent the night, leaving the next morning around sunrise.

After leaving, Charles McGill walked about for some time and, at noon, visited a pawnbrokers on Ontario Street, where he pawned his friend's coat for five dollars. He then purchased a revolver and some rounds. He was intent on getting Mary out of a life of prostitution. If she wouldn't leave with him, he'd kill himself, and hopefully that would convince her to choose another path, or so he later attested.

That afternoon, he returned to the house at 100 Cross Street and sat downstairs for some time with Mary Kelley and her friend, who also resided there. At one point, Mary went upstairs to change and invited Charles McGill to join her. Mary lay down on the bed and asked Charles to lie beside her. The two talked for about a half an hour, and Charles McGill tried to convince her to leave that house, but she refused, claiming that she'd been given fifteen dollars by a lake captain the previous Saturday, who'd also bought her a new dress. McGill pulled out the gun and placed it in his mouth

Illustrations of Charles McGill and Mary Kelley. *From the* Plain Dealer, *1879.*

but then turned it toward Mary, who was facing away from him. He pulled the trigger, shooting her once in the side of the head. At this, she screamed for someone to get a priest, turned to see McGill holding the revolver and begged him to forgive her. He then unloaded the rest of the bullets into her neck and chest. Every chamber being empty, he removed the spent rounds and loaded three more. Mary's body moved, and he continued to shoot her until the gun was again empty.

Afterward, in a very cool and collected manner, he strolled downstairs and washed himself. He was arrested and taken to jail, where he gave a statement to the coroner, which read:

> *Charles R. McGill sworn.*
> *My home is in Athens, Athens Co., Ohio where my mother lives. I have been living in Cleveland about a year and half. I have not been married with Mary Kelly. We have been living in the Atwater building as man and wife. That was last winter and not since then. We had to separate as we had nothing to live upon. I have been drinking very hard since the 13 day of October last up to Saturday then I did not drink much. I was informed that*

Mary Kelly was dead. I know who done it. I did. Never had the delirium tremens never drank to excess until October. I went up to commit suicide in her presence.
    Charles R. McGill

The body of Mary Kelley was conveyed to Cleveland's Woodland Cemetery, where she was laid to rest on December 4, 1877, in section B, lot 2, grave 15. After two trials, McGill was found guilty and was sentenced to death for the murder of twenty-five-year-old Mary Kelley. He was taken to the gallows and hanged on February 13, 1879. Immediately after the execution, McGill's body was sent directly to his mother's residence, where a wake and funeral were held. Charles R. McGill was interred in the West State Street Cemetery in Athens, Ohio. His epitaph reads:

"HANGED IN ACCORDANCE WITH LAW"
IN CLEVELAND. FOR THE MURDER
OF HIS SWEETHEART.

Following the grisly murder of Mary Kelley, Laura Lane moved away from the house, and it largely sat unoccupied for the next couple of years. It was rented occasionally, but the new tenants moved out shortly after moving in. In October 1879, there was a fire in the house that almost killed two occupants. The damage to the home was minimal, and soon after, a new tenant was found. In 1880, Laura Williams and her family took up residency on the second floor of 100 Cross Street but were completely unaware of its history and its otherworldly occupants.

Then, on December 2, 1881, that being the fourth anniversary of the murder, the haunting reemerged. Mary Lynch, Laura Williams's aunt, who occupied the room where the terrible deed was committed, awoke that night to extraordinary sounds and was paralyzed with fear as she observed two shadowy forms passing through the room. She could distinctly hear the rustling of clothes and the movement of furniture. Her niece, Laura Williams, also heard the sounds, as did Laura's son, Henry.

On other occasions, Henry Williams was witness to the ghostly manifestations of a man and a woman appearing in his bedroom. One night, he observed their misty forms standing in a distant corner across the room. He closed his eyes and, on opening them, found the spectral visitors standing beside his bed. More than once, he was so disturbed by the experiences that he had to leave his bed and stay elsewhere.

Charles R McGill sworn.

My home is in Athens, Athens Co Ohio where my Mother lives. I have been living in Cleveld about a year and half.

I have not been married with Mary Kelly. We have been living in the Atwater building as man and wife. that was last winter and not since then. we had to refferate as we had nothing to live upon. I have been drinking very hard since the 13 day of October last. up to Saturday then I did not drink much.. I was informed that Mary Kelly was dead. I know who done it. I did. never had the delerium tremens never drank to excess untill October. I went up to commit suicide in her presence.

Charles. R. McGill.

Charles McGill's confession letter. *Courtesy the Cuyahoga County Archives.*

Mary Lynch frequently found herself pinned to her bed as though she were being held down by some heavy, unseen force, which left her unable to speak or breathe. It was more than she could bear, and she ultimately moved out.

One night, Laura Williams said that she heard noises coming from her son's room and went in to investigate. She walked over to the window to make certain that it was securely closed, and a dark figure appeared, standing in the middle of the room. It moved aside to let her exit. A few nights later, some friends came over and were interrupted by the sound of someone walking around in the other room. The sound then transferred itself to walls of the room that the company sat in.

The following night, Laura Williams went to bed and awoke to someone opening her door, heavy footsteps crossing the room and the sound of someone sitting down in a chair. A few minutes later, the chair squeaked as though someone had just stood up from it. Footsteps crossed the room again and walked out.

One January night, Laura Williams left an oil lamp burning dimly on a table in her bedroom. As she lay in her bed in the gathering darkness, she watched as the flame on the wick flickered about. Suddenly, the flame extinguished itself, and the room was filled with a great, radiant glow. The sound of a silk dress moving about the room was heard making its way

The site of 100 Cross Street today. *Photo by William G. Krejci.*

over to the bedside, where it stopped. A moment later, an icy hand reached out and took hold of Mrs. Williams, who cried out to Mary Kelley, asking her what she wanted. At this, the hand withdrew itself. The rustling noise crossed the room and entered the closet. Three groans were heard, and the flame in the lamp reignited, filling the room with a warm glow once more.

Not long after, Laura Williams and her son moved out, and by 1885, they were residing on Cherry Street.

Quite recently, it has been suggested that McGill's grave itself is haunted. Originally, the haunting at West State Street Cemetery in Athens centered on a statue of an angel, dedicated to fallen Union soldiers from the Civil War. It is said that the statue has been seen with tears running down its face.

The house at 100 Cross Street was demolished around 1900 and was replaced by a small two-story commercial block. That structure, which bore the address 2607 to 2617 East 9th Street, was razed by 1932. Today, the site of 100 Cross Street is located at the side of the exit ramp from the eastbound lanes of Interstate 90 to Ontario Street.

CHAPTER 9

WOODLAND HILLS

41.48151, -81.60918

A look of solid grandeur, and of quiet antique glory,
Marks the quaint peaked attic windows and the wide substantial door;
People say "that house is haunted," but no weird or ghostly story
Pales the sunlight on the threshold, falling brightly as of yore.
—"The Phantom Ball" by Rosa Vertner Jeffrey

Situated on Cleveland's East Side, Woodland Hills Avenue was a rural road running north and south that had few residences located on it. The area was, by most accounts, a relatively quiet and drowsy part of town. It stands to reason, then, that those who dwelt in the area were surprised to learn that a home in their locale was the scene of a reported haunting. On Wednesday, November 26, 1884, the *Cleveland Leader* made the announcement that a house on Woodland Hills Avenue was being haunted by unearthly screams, white figures and mysterious red lights.

According to the article, the house in question was a two-story frame dwelling that sat close to the roadside, southeast of the intersection of Woodland and Woodland Hills Avenues. Two weeks earlier, another newspaper ran a story of an abandoned haunted house located near that intersection. This house being the only one fitting the description, it started to draw curiosity seekers.

About a week after that article appeared, a group of ten Woodland Avenue streetcar conductors, headed by twenty-six-year-old William J. Couch, made a search of the house. Six men remained outside while the other four boldly entered. The men, armed only with lanterns, made a thorough search for hidden rooms where ghosts or goblins might hide, but no such chambers were found. As the men were preparing to depart, their lanterns suddenly went out and a loud moan echoed through the empty rooms. They hastily fled the house, and the sound followed them a good distance. All ten conductors vowed that they would never go hunting for ghosts again.

On Saturday, November 22, Andrew Belden, who lived next door to the haunted house, entered the property with his hired man. The two proceeded to the cellar, where they commenced to dig a number of holes. Belden claimed that he and his man unearthed many small bones and a silver ring marked with the letter *D*. The bones, he said, were delivered to a local chemist for analysis.

The following night, a farmer named James Wilson was riding in the vicinity of the haunted house on his way home. The horse clip-clopped passed the storied building as Wilson cast brief, wary glances at it. Suddenly, the windows were filled with eerie red lights, and Wilson saw ghostly white figures moving about inside, as though engaged in some dance of the dead. This terrified not only Wilson but also his horse, which threw him to the ground and ran off.

At eleven thirty the following Monday night, several boys were returning home from the opera. Their journey brought them past the house, where they observed a figure draped in white digging in the backyard. Startled by the apparition, the boys screamed, and the figure ascended into the air and vanished. They turned and ran home, telling their parents what they'd seen. Two of their fathers, those being Mr. Morton and Mr. Lefner, armed themselves and returned to the house but could find no digging implements or signs that the earth in the backyard had been disturbed. Throngs of people visited the site the next day, where wild and exaggerated stories began to circulate.

That Friday, a crowd of about fifty men was gathered near the haunted house when they were charged by a wildly snorting cow. It was said to be mounted by a misty, sepulchral white figure. The men stood firmly on the muddy, partially frozen and slush-covered road as the figure approached. The phantom rider then drew back its arm and hurled at them a glowing ball of fire. At this, the men turned and ran off screaming. One glanced back to see the road completely empty and only the barren snowy landscape behind him.

Meanwhile, the *Plain Dealer* reported that the haunting was a hoax, claiming that it was attracting crowds of men and boys who were breaking

THAT GHOST.

More Disturbance Reported on Woodland Hills Avenue.

Red Lights, Unearthly Screams and White Figures in Endless Confusion.

A headline reporting on the haunting near Woodland Hills. *From the* Cleveland Leader, *1884.*

down doors and smashing windows. The vandals were tearing down the fence to feed a fire they'd lit in the road to keep warm. When they had tired of stoning the reported haunted house, they turned their attention to neighboring houses and took aim at those. By this point, the story was being carried by out-of-state newspapers, and travelers to Cleveland arrived at their hotels and asked for directions to the haunted house.

A wild story of the house's history was also starting to circulate. The haunted house, as the legend claimed, was said to have been built by a man named Davidson, who died in 1863. It was then used by another family as a farmhouse until 1872. Afterward, the farm was subdivided into city lots until only the little house on the small location remained. For the next eight years, it was rented out to various tenants, and in 1880, occupation was taken up by an elderly spiritualistic medium named Hollister. This man had a grown daughter who assisted him with nightly séances. One day, the daughter disappeared. It was believed that she'd eloped with a man from the West, but Hollister never spoke of the matter. In time, he ceased holding séances and withdrew into his home, shutting himself off from the rest of the world. After he'd not been seen for a number of days, police were called to check on him and found the man hanging from a beam in the rafters of the attic. No suicide note was ever found. The body was not in the ground long before it was disinterred and delivered to the dissecting tables of the medical college, or so the stories said.

Reporters looked further into this legend and the house itself. Things just didn't seem to square up. From what they could tell through simple observation, there was no cellar from which one could dig up bones or a silver ring. Furthermore, the attic of the house wasn't nearly large enough to accommodate a suicidal spiritualist. The location of the house was also clarified as being on Woodland Avenue, just beyond the convent for the Sisters of Notre Dame, not on Woodland Hills Avenue, as the initial reports claimed. The house in question was owned by a man named Samuel Baldwin, who stated that the house was only a few years old.

Samuel Griffin Baldwin was born on October 12, 1806, to Wyllys and Phoebe Eisner Baldwin of Schuyler County, New York. The eldest of nine, Samuel Baldwin left his home for Cleveland in 1840, where he studied law and was admitted to the bar. Rather than following a career in that field, he turned his attention to property investments and soon amassed a great fortune. On September 3, 1843, he was married to Susan Lambert. They had no biological children but adopted a son and a daughter.

The property where this house existed was situated on the southeast corner of lot 426 in Newburgh Township and comprised five acres of land. It had been purchased in 1852 by Dr. William Alleyne Nicholson from Patrick and Sally Thomas, as part of the Rudolph Edwards estate. Dr. Nicholson died on March 10, 1853, and his wife, Elizabeth, returned to New York four years later, where she married Reverend William Ives Budington. They sold the property to Valentine Clark on March 29, 1867. It was sold three more times over the next two years before it came into the hands of Samuel Baldwin in 1869. It should be noted that no Davidsons or Hollisters appear anywhere in the title transfers.

By 1874, there were two structures on the property, though the newspaper stated that the house was only a few years old. At the time of the reported haunting, Samuel Baldwin was living at 177 St. Clair in Cleveland, this presently being the northwest corner of East 3rd and St. Clair. Until about a month earlier, the house had been rented out to the foreman of the city scavengers, who left it to live closer to town.

By all appearances, the neighbors seemed to have had enough of the haunted house business, and many complaints were lodged with the authorities. On December 2, 1884, Lieutenant Tompkins of the Cleveland Police detailed

The site of the haunted house near Woodland Hills is an empty lot today. *Photo by William G. Krejci.*

Sergeant Bradly and two patrolmen to watch the house and prevent further damage. Also watching the house was a General Elwell, who announced that he would shoot any prowlers caught on the property. This seemed to do the trick. No further mention of the haunting can be found afterward.

So, what became of the haunted house?

Samuel Baldwin's wife, Susan, died in 1890. The following June, he married Carrie Schwabb, who'd been living as a member of his household. Samuel Griffin Baldwin died on February 22, 1893, and the house and property passed to his second wife.

Originally situated on what was called Woodland Avenue, by 1910, the house was listed with the address 10806 South Woodland Avenue and was being rented to the Jakubovsky family. In 1913, that part of Newburgh was incorporated into Cleveland and the name of the street was changed to Buckeye. With that, the house's address was changed to 11006. Then, as new houses were built to the east, the addresses were adjusted, and the house was renumbered 10914 Buckeye Road.

Around 1920, Carrie Baldwin sold the property and the Jakubovsky family moved out. The house was torn down about ten years later.

Today, the site of the house sits in the heart of the Woodland Hills neighborhood, also called Buckeye-Woodhill. Currently, the site is occupied by a vacant lot on the south side of Buckeye Road between East 111th Street and Martin Luther King Jr. Drive.

CHAPTER 10
THE SHIPHERD SUICIDE

41.50204, -81.66142

O'er all there hung the shadow of a fear,
A sense of mystery the spirit daunted,
And said, as plain as whisper in the ear,
The place is haunted.
—*"The Haunted House" by Thomas Hood*

Just as the tale of the haunted house near Woodland Hills was unfolding, another story of a haunted house in Cleveland surfaced. Apparently, Cleveland could only handle one ghost story at a time, as no reports of this other haunting were carried in local newspapers. It first appeared in the *New York Times* on December 1, 1884, and from there spread to various papers across the nation.

The house where all this transpired was a large stone mansion on Prospect Street, which was built around 1876 by Charles H. Bulkley, a publisher and father of later Senator Robert J. Bulkley, who was born in there in 1880. On completion, the home carried the address 459 Prospect. The Bulkleys occasionally rented out the house, and on February 2, 1884, they sold it to Frances and James Shipherd.

James Raymond Shipherd was born on April 14, 1835, to Dr. John Jay and Esther Raymond Shipherd of Oberlin, Ohio. His father, a Congregational minister, was a cofounder of Oberlin College and founded Olivet College in Michigan. Following his father's death, James Shipherd moved to Cleveland, where he found employment as a salesman with the dry goods and millinery

The Shipherd House in 1973. *Photo courtesy Cleveland Public Library Photograph Collection.*

firm of Judd and Coffin. Soon after, he was admitted as a partner in the firm of Morgan, Root and Shipherd. In 1860, he was married to Frances Barker. Within a few years, he struck out and established his own millinery, but around 1880, he accepted the position of superintendent of the millinery department in the firm of E.M. McGillin and Company.

On June 27, 1884, James Shipherd was caught embezzling money from his employer. He was charged and convicted that July and was sentenced to ten days in the workhouse. For a time after this, he considered relocating to another city but instead looked at returning to the industry he loved and put plans in motion to reopen his own millinery.

On September 1, 1884, ownership of the Shipherd mansion, which now carried the address 909 Prospect Street, was transferred to Mary McGillin, the wife of Edward M. McGillin, his former employer. This was done to settle the matter of what Shipherd still owed to the company from what he had illegally taken. Shipherd also started to move into the location of his new millinery, but a few days after moving in, he met with a number of businessmen he regularly consulted with and they strongly dissuaded him from following through with the venture. This seemed to dishearten him and completely break his spirit.

In the early morning hours of September 12, 1884, Shipherd quietly ascended the stairs to the attic and entered the unfurnished room at the front of the house, which was used for storage. He barricaded the door with a heavy box of stained glass that had been kept in that room, then pulled out a heavy cedar chest and mounted it. He withdrew a length of sturdy cord, tied it around the rafter above him and, from this, ended his life. His hanging body was discovered shortly after by his wife, who went looking for him when he didn't come down for breakfast.

The body of James R. Shipherd was laid to rest at Woodland Cemetery two days later but was relocated to Lake View Cemetery in 1907. Within a month of her husband's suicide, Frances Shipherd moved out of the Prospect Street residence.

And then the house was empty.

Rather than take up residence in the former Shipherd home, the McGillins chose to rent out the house. By what was related next, finding

The unfurnished front room of the attic where James R. Shipherd ended his life. *Photo by William G. Krejci.*

The Shipherd House. It looks very much the same today. *Photo by William G. Krejci.*

a tenant proved rather difficult. The *New York Times* reported that a "reputable gentleman" from Cleveland claimed that the former home of James Shipherd was haunted.

Late one afternoon, a married couple came to view the house. After thoroughly examining the kitchen and parlors, they started to ascend the staircase when they heard a groaning sound. Leaving his wife downstairs, the man followed the noise up to the attic. On entering the front room, he was horrified to see a man hanging from the rafter. He ran over to cut the man down, but as he approached, the man vanished before his eyes. When he returned to his wife at the foot of the stairs, she noticed that her husband was visibly shaken. He made an excuse, and the two hastily departed. When they reached their carriage, he told her that the house was not the right one for them.

Not long after, another man came to view the house with a friend. As the men examined the downstairs rooms, they heard the sound of someone walking above them. Thinking that someone else might be viewing the house, they made their way up to the attic. They entered the front room and discovered a man sitting on a cedar chest with his back to them. A moment later, he vanished. Thinking it some kind of a trick, the two men inspected the attic and the trunk but could find no trace of the man. It should be noted that the trunk was the same cedar chest from which James Shipherd was said to have taken his leap into eternity.

A hired man who worked for one of the neighbors was said to have had a similar experience. Having been sent into the house for one reason or another, he also witnessed the vanishing man in the attic. Stories of the haunting were whispered among the neighbors, and children, in passing the house, would quickly scurry to the other side of the street. The same held true for many adults.

By all appearances, a number of years passed, and no tenant could be found. Edward McGillin briefly resided in the house in 1888, then abruptly sold it that same year to George E. Anderson. Even at that, the house remained unoccupied until the mid-1890s.

In 1906, the address was changed to 3657 Prospect, and it still carries that address today. As time elapsed, the house's haunted reputation was forgotten, and the ghost of James R. Shipherd seemed to vanish from all memory. Well recorded here is the historic haunting of that beautiful Cleveland brownstone, but one has to wonder in passing—is it haunted still?

CHAPTER 11
PATRICK SMITH'S HAUNTED HOUSES

WASHINGTON STREET: 41.49259, -81.70862
CRAWFORD ROAD: 41.50892, -81.62698
LAKE STREET: 41.50551, -81.69209
ERIE STREET: 41.50421, -81.69003

I know not how it was, but, with the first glimpse of the building, a sense of insufferable gloom pervaded my spirit.
—"The Fall of the House of Usher" by Edgar Allan Poe

Late November and early December 1884 really seemed to be the time to bring Cleveland's ghost stories to light. It didn't end with Samuel Baldwin's house on Woodland or the Shipherd residence on Prospect. Cleveland city councilman Patrick Smith felt that the time had come for him to step forward and share *his* experiences with haunted houses. After all, he was the proud owner of four such buildings.

Patrick Smith, to begin with, was born in Bailieboro, County Cavan, Ireland, on March 17, 1827. He came to Cleveland with his parents in 1836, but after a few years, the family relocated to Independence Road in Newburgh. It was there that the youngster first gained an interest in the river and its operations. In 1843, he took a job on a river dredge in Cleveland, and the following year, he purchased that dredge. Over the next few years, he purchased a few tugs, and before long, he'd amassed one of the largest tug fleets on the Great Lakes. This, along with his land investments, eventually made him one of the richest men in Cleveland.

On October 28, 1851, Patrick Smith was married to Margaret Olwill of New York, with whom he fathered eight children. Margaret died on June 26, 1887, and he was next married to Mary F. Burns on August 20, 1888.

HAUNTED HOUSES.

Cleveland Man Has a Peculiar Mania for Them.

Lived in Them During the Past Twenty-Five Years

And Has Never Seen a Ghost.

A headline reports on Patrick Smith and his haunted houses. *From the* Plain Dealer, *1897.*

For many years, he served as a Cleveland city councilman, a member of the board of the city waterworks and even, for a term, as county commissioner.

So why would a man such as this show any interest in haunted houses?

The answer was a simple one: they were cheap. Whenever Smith heard about a supposed haunted house being up for sale, he'd come in and scoop it up for a much-discounted price.

At the time of going public with his haunted houses, Patrick Smith and his family were residing in an aged, redbrick home on the northwest corner of Washington and Pearl Streets. Situated on a large and beautiful tract of land, the house was counted as one of the richest on the city's West Side. Carrying

Patrick Smith. *From* A History of the City of Cleveland, *1897.*

the address 224 Washington, it was a three-story affair, with a two-story servants' wing at the back. Above the mansard walls, the house was crowned with a six-foot ironclad cupola. It was said of the old house that, by its appearance, it seemed such a place as might be the resort of a dozen ghosts. The rooms were large and full of little nooks and corners where any number of otherworldly beings might hide.

For many years, stories circulated of how unearthly noises were often heard issuing from the house. Strange lights were also seen to move about the mansion. Most recognizable from outside was the "haunted room." This was easily identified by a pair of windows that constantly had the blinds closed. Many neighbors believed that the Smiths dared not enter that room, while children in the neighborhood refused to walk past that part of the house after dark. Patrick Smith believed that the sounds heard in the house, prior to his purchasing it, were caused by a man who broke in during the middle of the night and dragged a heavy chain up and down the stairs.

Legend states that the house had been the scene of some grisly crime and that the poor restless spirit of the victim wandered the old halls and corridors at night. The history of the place speaks a little differently.

West Village was laid out on the west bank of the flats and included, within its boundaries, the area along the bluffs just above. This was many years before the establishment of Ohio City. In 1833, the Buffalo Company, which owned and subdivided West Village, contracted one lot to a man named Orin Smith—no relation to Patrick Smith. In turn, the contract was taken over by Charles Standart of Milan, Ohio. At that time, his brother, Needham Maynard Standart, had relocated to Cleveland to organize a shipbuilding firm with a man named David Griffith. After a lengthy stay at the Franklin House, Needham Standart realized that a more permanent residence was needed. Thus, in 1836, he commenced construction of the brick house on his brother's lot at the northwest corner of Washington and Pearl Streets. In a few short years, Needham Standart built his fortune. Aside from shipbuilding, he engaged in banking, beef packing and salt and produce shipping. He also served as mayor of Ohio City, all while residing in that brick house that would one day gain fame as being haunted.

In 1842, Needham Standart purchased a property on Detroit Street, near the western outskirts of Ohio City, and built a new house, which history would come to call Needham Castle. Five years later, his brother sold the house on Washington to Luther and Arvilla Moses, who only owned it for four years. It briefly passed into the hands of Benjamin and Nancy Jones and, two years later, was sold to James Hobart Ford and his wife, Arabella.

Needham Maynard Standart, circa 1835. *Photo courtesy Milan Museum.*

The Fords resided in the house until around 1860, at which time they moved west. On the outbreak of the U.S. Civil War, James Ford was appointed captain and raised a unit of volunteers in the Colorado Territory. He was soon after promoted to colonel and, before the end of the war, was made brevet brigadier general of the U.S. Volunteers. Ford County, Kansas, is named in his honor.

In 1863, James and Arabella Ford sold their Cleveland house to a harness maker named John G. Haserot, who only resided in the house for about a year. Haserot's son, Frank, built a fortune in the canned goods industry. His company exists today as Northern Haserot, and his grave at Lake View Cemetery is marked by the famous Haserot Angel statue. Officially called *The Angel of Death Victorious*, the statue depicts a winged angel extinguishing a large torch. Natural aging has caused a patina that gives the appearance of tears streaming from its eyes. Some have even suggested that the statue itself is haunted.

The house on Washington and Pearl next passed into the hands of William Vorce in 1864, who, in turn, rented it to his son, LaFayette, and LaFayette's wife, child and in-laws.

LaFayette Vorce came to Cleveland from New York in 1854 at the age of twenty. He attended the Commercial College in Cleveland, then entered into the wholesale grocery and commission trade. In 1858, he was married to Juliette Newton, with whom he had a son named William.

LaFayette Vorce and his family didn't reside long in that house on Washington and Pearl. He died there on June 15, 1864, from consumption. The funeral was held from the residence, but his burial was at the family plot in Westfield, New York.

For the next two years, following the death of LaFayette Vorce, the house sat empty and alone. Here, rumors of the haunting began to spread. When word reached Patrick Smith about the haunted house on Washington being available for purchase, he jumped at the opportunity. A friend warned him not to purchase it, saying that he wouldn't last long in the place, but Smith was determined to have it, as it was large and quite comfortable—to him, at least. He purchased it from William Vorce for $5,000, knowing that he wouldn't be able to sell it for ten cents on the dollar owing to its haunted reputation. A neighbor who lived across the street said that he would gladly have purchased it, were it not for the ghosts.

At the time of purchasing the Washington Street house, Patrick Smith was living on the East Side on Crawford Road. He'd purchased that house for the same reason he acquired the one on Washington. It, too, could be had at a much-reduced price, owing to its haunted reputation. According to Smith, no one would have it, as no one wanted to live in the same dwelling as a ghost.

That house had been built around 1843 by Benjamin and Sophronia Welch on property purchased from Benjamin's brother, John. The home that the Welches built was a frame structure, located near the southeast corner of present-day Hough Avenue and Crawford Road, in what was at that time East Cleveland Township. In 1853, the Welches took over operation of Dunham Tavern on Euclid Avenue, and the property was sold to their son-in-law, James B. Wilbur, who remained until 1859.

The house changed hands frequently over the next few years until ultimately coming into the possession of Patrick Smith in 1864. He purchased it from a man named Alden Stockwell for $4,000. It's uncertain why the house would have had the reputation of being haunted. Aside from changing hands through a series of brief owners, and likely being unoccupied during that time, there's no record of any tragedies or deaths occurring there.

The Crawford Road house stood until around 1890, at which time the lot was subdivided and a neighborhood sprang up in its place. The site is currently the parking lot just north of the African American Museum at 1765 Crawford Road.

During the late 1890s, Patrick Smith again spoke of his haunted houses. He claimed two more had been in his possession. According to Smith, he'd bought them because they were cheap and because he wanted to see a ghost. Both houses were located downtown.

The first of these stood at 177 Lake Street, later numbered 319 Lake. Smith purchased it from Azariah Everett for $4,500 at just about the same time

A view along Crawford Road, circa 1890. *Photo courtesy Cleveland Public Library Photograph Collection.*

that he was buying the Crawford Road property. This was a two-story brick structure that had been built in the early 1850s by Marcus West. In 1855, the building was sold to Harvey Hunt, who, three years later, conveyed it to Mr. Everett. By all appearances, Everett rented out the house, as city directories indicate that he lived on Superior during the time of his ownership.

It seems that Smith himself only resided in the house very briefly. This was in 1866, just after he purchased the Washington Street house and moved out of the one on Crawford. In 1876, Patrick and Margaret Smith transferred ownership of the Lake Street house to their daughter, Estella. In later years, the house was acquired by the City of Cleveland and was demolished to make way for Willard Park at the northwest corner of East 9th Street and Lakeside Avenue. The Cleveland Fire Fighters' Memorial stands on the former site of that house. The Free Stamp sits about seventy-five feet to the west.

The other house was located a little to the south of this, directly on the northeast corner of St. Clair and Erie Streets. It was a smaller, two-story brick house with a basement. Patrick Smith purchased it in 1877 for $6,400 from William Quigley, administrator of the estate of the late John Smyth. At the time, the house carried the address 80 Erie Street, which, in 1886, was changed to 131 Erie. In 1906, the address was again changed, renumbered as 1317 East 9th Street.

This house's haunted reputation reached back to at least fifteen years before Smith made his purchase. This was the same house where, on November 25, 1862, two girls witnessed the Erie Street Ghost looking down at them from an upper-chamber window. According to reports, the scene distressed one of the girls so severely that she fell into convulsions.

In the years after Patrick Smith's ownership, the building served as Kerner's Saloon, Annabelle's Restaurant, Smith's Oldtimers Cafe and, finally, as the Seaway Bar and Lounge. It was torn down in 1962, and the lot was incorporated into the Erieview plan for downtown Cleveland. In 1987, the Galleria at Erieview was built on the site.

Patrick Smith owned many other properties around town, but these are the four that he claimed to be haunted. On his retirement from the dredge and towing industry, Patrick Smith handed over the reins of his company to his sons Louis and James. He devoted much of his time thereafter to supporting various charitable causes.

On Wednesday, May 7, 1902, Patrick Smith was injured in a streetcar accident at the west end of the Superior Viaduct. While riding in his buggy, he crossed into the path of the trolley, and the back of the buggy was struck, throwing Smith to the ground. He suffered no broken bones

The site of Patrick Smith's haunted house on the northwest corner of Pearl and Washington today. *Photo by William G. Krejci.*

but received a severe gash to the back of his head. Though the wounds weren't fatal in the moment, he never recovered from the shock and died on Sunday morning, May 11, 1902, at his storied home on Washington Street. Patrick Smith was buried that Tuesday in his family plot at St. John Cemetery on Woodland Avenue.

Following his death, Patrick Smith's haunted house on Washington passed into the hands of his daughter, Estella Cunnea. In 1906, the address was changed to 2504 Washington Avenue. It was rented out to various tenants, being used briefly as an office for the A. MacDougall Company in 1937. The following year, it was again used as a residence. In late 1938, it was purchased by the board of county commissioners and was torn down the following year to make way for the Main Avenue Bridge over the Cuyahoga River. Today, the site of that grand home is occupied by an overpass for the Shoreway at the corner of West 25th Street and Washington Avenue.

In sharing the story of his haunted house on Washington Street, Patrick Smith once related how two priests had come to him and offered to drive the ghosts out of that house. He earnestly wished that he would see a ghost. He'd been looking for one for more than fifty years, but alas, a spectral visit to the sturdy tug master was never to be.

CHAPTER 12

CONVENT OF THE POOR CLARES

41.49514, −81.67486

And are you prepared to encounter all the horrors that a building such as "what
one reads about" may produce? Have you a stout heart?
—Northanger Abbey *by Jane Austen*

The year 1884 couldn't close without just one more Cleveland ghost
story. This one centered itself on a home that, at the time the story
was reported, was occupied by a religious order.

The house referred to here was located at 323 Perry Street, later carrying
the address 246 Perry, then 2480 East 22nd Street. Situated just north of St.
Bridget's Roman Catholic Church, it was a large, four-story brick house that
boasted fourteen rooms. In 1884, the building was occupied by the Little
Sisters of the Poor, and the house served as the Convent of the Poor Clares.
Many years earlier, the large structure was home to the McCurdy family.

Alexander Lynde McCurdy was born on July 19, 1804, in Lyme,
Connecticut, to Richard and Ursula McCurdy. He was married to Josephine
Lord in 1834 and with her had five children. Immediately following their
nuptials, Alexander and Josephine McCurdy moved to Cleveland and settled
on a farm in Newburgh Township.

On May 24, 1852, Alexander McCurdy purchased lots 3 and 4 of
Edward Scoville's subdivision for $1,350. According to tax records,
McCurdy sat on the property for some time before making improvements.
In 1860, the large mansion was added to the site. The family hadn't
lived in the home long before tragedy struck. On November 26, 1861,

An undated view of St. Bridget's Church. The McCurdy House appears to the right. *Cleveland State University. Michael Schwartz Library.*

Alexander and Josephine's ten-year-old daughter, Alexanna, died from diphtheria. The funeral was held at the home, and interment took place at Woodland Cemetery.

Then, in July 1866, Alexander and Josephine's twenty-two-year-old daughter, Catherine, traveled east to visit family in Connecticut and recover her health, which had been failing as of late. At that same time, her mother had also been in poor health. Sadly, Catherine McCurdy's condition continued to deteriorate, and while in Connecticut, she passed away, her death occurring in early August that year. News of Catherine's passing was kept from her mother. Josephine McCurdy joined her daughter in death only a few days later, passing away on August 8, 1866. Both were interred beside Alexanna at Woodland Cemetery.

Two years later, the house was put up for rent with an option to purchase. Mortimer E. Hart, McCurdy's son-in-law, assisted with making arrangements to rent out the house. In 1872, Alexander McCurdy moved to Santa Barbara, California, but occasionally returned to Cleveland during the summer months.

In 1874, the McCurdy home was modernized with gaslights and indoor plumbing. It was then converted into a boardinghouse and took on many tenants. It was while the home was serving in this capacity that the ghost stories emerged.

During that time, it was reported that strange lights were seen in the windows. Witnesses also claimed to see white-robed figures, unearthly forms with eyes of fire, pacing through its halls at night. Shrieks and groans were said to be heard throughout the large mansion. These stories created intense excitement, and the more the matter was investigated, the more mysterious it became. Hundreds of people congregated about the place at night, watching and waiting for the apparitions to make an appearance.

While serving as a boardinghouse, the building saw one more death, the passing of eight-year-old Georgie Emma Bean, the only daughter of Dr. John and Lillis Bean, on October 19, 1875. The cause of death was scarlet fever. The funeral was held at their home, and burial took place at Woodland Cemetery, though her remains were moved to Lake View Cemetery in 1902.

It was said that a man named White was in charge of the estate and that he tried in vain to dispose of the property, but no one would take it at any price. Finally, the strange occurrences ceased. The neighborhood resumed its ordinary quietude, and White succeeded in selling the property, though at a great financial sacrifice.

The site of the McCurdy House today. *Photo by William G. Krejci.*

That last part of the tale turned out to be inaccurate. Alexander L. McCurdy handled the sale of the estate himself. He sold his house on Perry Street to Kilian Schlosser on December 1, 1880, for $10,500. Six years later, McCurdy passed away at his home in Santa Barbara.

In December 1881, Kilian Schlosser sold the Perry Street house, for the same price he'd paid for it, to the Friars Minor of the Order of St. Francis of Cleveland, who in turn used it as the Convent of the Poor Clares. The house was added onto extensively during that time to accommodate its new purpose. The Poor Clares used the building for more than twenty years, and in 1905, it was sold to the Shields & Wertheim Company, a cigar manufacturer, which used the building as their production factory.

On the morning of January 12, 1918, the building was heavily damaged by a raging inferno. Firefighting efforts were hampered by high winds and freezing temperatures. Also damaged was St. Bridget's Catholic Church to the south and St. John's Greek Catholic Church immediately to the north. Though the damage was extensive, Shields & Wertheim managed to save the building. Soon after making repairs, the company relocated to

Woodland Avenue, and the building sat empty until 1926, at which time it was taken over by the Novelty Lighting Corporation. The back half of the building was occupied by the Acme Textile Mill Ends Company.

In 1961, Novelty Lighting relocated to Broadway, and soon after, the building was demolished. Currently, the site is occupied by a grassy lot near the southwest corner of Community College Avenue and East 22nd Street.

CHAPTER 13

THE CLEVELAND MEDICAL COLLEGE GRAVEYARD

41.50412, -81.68930

Who shall conceive the horrors of my secret toil,
as I dabbled among the unhallowed damps of the grave,
or tortured the living animal to animate the lifeless clay?
—Frankenstein; or, The Modern Prometheus
by Mary Wollstonecraft Shelley

Looking back two chapters, the reader will recall that one of Patrick Smith's haunted houses sat at the northeast corner of East 9th Street and St. Clair Avenue. At that house, in 1862, two girls were terrified by the Erie Street Ghost. Curiously, another haunted site was located directly across St. Clair Avenue on the grounds of the Cleveland Medical College. That ghost story emerged in mid-June 1885.

The first medical college building to grace the site was erected in 1843. The land and building funds were acquired through the generous contributions of various citizens of Cleveland. Founded by the faculty members of a medical college that existed at Willoughby, it was established and operated under charter by the medical department of Western Reserve University, now Case Western Reserve University, which was then located in Hudson. From that institution emerged University Hospitals of Cleveland.

Plans to replace the original medical college building with a new one were put in motion in 1884, and demolition of the old building commenced in March the following year. That June, during the excavation, a gruesome discovery was made when a series of burial vaults were unearthed.

The Cleveland Medical College, circa 1880. *Photo courtesy Cleveland Public Library Photograph Collection.*

Shortly after the medical college was opened in 1843, a number of pits, some more than twenty feet deep, were dug into the ground behind it. These were located at the northeast corner of the lot. Large wooden barrels were then placed in these holes, stacked end to end, one on top of the other, with the tops and bottoms knocked out. When students were done dissecting a cadaver for medical study, those remains were unceremoniously disposed of by being dumped into these deep vaults. Chloride of lime, and other disinfectants, were thrown on top to prevent the buildup of noxious odors and gasses. This went on for more than forty years.

When excavation for the new medical school building commenced, these burial vaults were opened, and a ghastly scene unfolded. Reeking masses of half-decomposed flesh and entrails were fished out of the vats. Some of the bodies dumped into the deep vaults had been treated with arsenic to preserve the remains during dissection. These were practically embalmed and were brought up in a condition very near to that in which they were deposited on the site many years earlier.

As the remains were removed, a sickeningly nauseating smell permeated the area and could be detected more than half a mile away. Nearby residents were forced to close their doors and windows, while others were compelled to leave the area entirely, seeking fresh air in a park located in another part of town. Many businesses had to close on account of the stench.

Aside from the remains that were pulled from the vaults, a number of other burials were located on the site. Some complete bodies were excavated during the day but were quickly covered with sand until they could be removed under the cover of night. The unearthing of these graves, in spite of the smell, drew a large crowd of curiosity seekers. The scene also drew reports of ghostly activity. It was said that phantom figures were seen to move about the disturbed graves—the restless spirits of those who had been interred there, no doubt. Those who had ghoulishly descended on the site during the day to witness the macabre spectacle of unearthing graves were replaced around midnight by those hoping to catch a glimpse of the ghostly apparitions.

Ultimately, the upper portions of the vaults, along with their grisly contents, were removed from the site by a contractor named Dart. These were taken by wagon down to the docks, loaded onto a scow and, from there, taken out onto the lake. The barrels and remains were then dumped overboard and sank to the dark and murky depths of Lake Erie. The lower barrels that were located at the bottom of the pits were left in place with the remains they contained, as a festering mass of corruption, to await the end of eternity, in the place they were consigned to so many years earlier.

The new medical college building that went up in 1885 remained on the site until 1922. That year, a new school of medicine was built at 2109 Adelbert Road, and the facility on St. Clair and East 9th was demolished. The site of the old medical college graveyard is currently occupied by

One Cleveland Center stands on the former site of the Cleveland Medical College. *Photo by William G. Krejci.*

the northeast corner of the One Cleveland Center plaza. It's very likely that the bodies at the bottom of the vaults, as the reports of 1885 suggest, still take their repose at that site and will continue to do so until the end of days.

CHAPTER 14

THE GHOST SHRIEKS

BLAIR'S BLOCK: 41.49807, -81.69050
HEFFRON'S UNDERTAKER'S PARLOR: 41.49141, -81.70794

"Oh whence do you come, my dear friend, to me,
With your golden hair all fallen below your knee,
And your face as white as snowdrops on the lea,
And your voice as hollow as the hollow sea?"
"From the other world I come back to you:
My locks are uncurled with dripping drenching dew,
You know the old, whilst I know the new:
But to-morrow you shall know this too."
—*"The Poor Ghost" by Christina Rossetti*

In January 1886, another ghost story started making its way around Cleveland. The appearance of that ghost was believed to be connected to the death of a woman at a boardinghouse on Prospect.

The site of the boardinghouse was originally occupied by Mrs. J. Young's bathhouse. On hand was a physician named D.T. Kramer, who offered "electro-thermal" curative baths. Then, in 1870, Henry Blair purchased the lot, demolished the bathhouse and put up a commercial building that he named Blair's Block. It first carried the address 36 Prospect Street, but by the time that the story was unfolding, it had been changed to 54 Prospect. It was a three-story brick building with a basement. The first floor housed various businesses, while the two upper floors contained fourteen rooms and were used to accommodate boarders.

There was nothing unique or out of the ordinary about the place until the story of the haunting emerged. The events leading up to that extraordinary chapter in Cleveland history unfolded thus.

Emily Dallyn was born in 1844 in Devon, England, to Joseph and Maria Dallyn. When she was a little girl, the family relocated to Hamilton, Ontario, where, in 1871, Emily was married to William John Frayne. The Dallyn family operated a bellows-making factory, but when Emily's father passed away in 1878, William Frayne took over the operation. He died in September 1884.

Being very much grief-stricken over the loss of her husband, Emily Frayne sought the company of her sister, Emma Hatton, who resided in Cleveland. She wrote in August 1885 and expressed her wish to come and visit. She arrived in a very low state of health on Sunday, January 3, 1886, and planned for an extensive stay with her sister's family, who resided on the third floor, in room 10, of Blair's Block.

Over the course of the week that followed, Emily Frayne fainted several times but, after a few moments, rallied her strength and, in no time, had recovered. On Thursday, she was outside playing with her little niece and even felt well enough to run a race against her. That evening, while in the hallway outside the apartment, Emily Frayne collapsed and was carried to bed. Emma Hatton sent for the doctor, but he wasn't at home. Emily Frayne was made comfortable and, before long, had fallen asleep. The family retired to bed but were awakened around three o'clock in the morning by the sound of Emily Frayne violently retching. Medical assistance was again called for, but before the doctor arrived, Emily Frayne passed away.

It was first thought that her symptoms resembled those of a poisoning victim, and her sister believed that she may have either attempted suicide by swallowing poison or swallowed some by mistake. Coroner George W. West examined the remains and concluded the cause of death to be heart disease.

It was reported soon after that at the moment of Emily Frayne's death, a curious supernatural incident occurred in neighboring room 14, which was occupied by a thirty-two-year-old fresco painter named Frank Lamb. Lamb had been out for the evening and returned late, going to sleep sometime after midnight. He was awakened a couple of hours later to the feeling of someone grasping him firmly. He turned over to see a beautiful woman of about the age of twenty, with long blonde hair and a flowing dress with red, yellow and green printed flowers, sitting on the sofa a few feet away. The dress, he claimed, was reminiscent of those that were in vogue about fifteen years earlier.

A view of Prospect Avenue, circa 1899. *Photo courtesy Cleveland Public Library Photograph Collection.*

After a few moments, Lamb asked the young woman what she wanted. The woman simply extended her right hand and shushed him. At this, she vanished. Lamb said that he wasn't afraid in the least and was inclined to chalk the whole thing up to a bad dream. He rolled over and tried to fall back to sleep, but about ten minutes later, he heard footsteps cross the room and approach the other side of his bed. Whatever it was seized his bedclothes and mattress and threw him onto the floor. Thinking an intruder had entered the room and accosted him, he pulled himself up from the floor, swinging and swearing, but realized immediately that he was entirely alone. He checked the door and found it still locked.

On opening the door, he was met by a neighbor named William Rice, who occupied the next room. Rice had been awakened by the commotion coming from Lamb's room and, thinking he had struggled with an intruder, inquired about what was going on. For reasons that he could never explain, Lamb told him that there was nothing amiss in *his* room, but rather the trouble was in the Hattons' apartment. At that very moment, Emma Hatton stepped out into the hall with tears in her eyes, exclaiming that her sister had just died. Lamb returned to his room and found his sheets and blankets twisted into a cone-shaped pile in the middle of the floor.

The room below Lamb's was occupied by the McDonald family. Mrs. McDonald was likewise awakened by the sound of Lamb striking the floor. Being of the same mind as Rice, she thought to assist, but on reaching the door, she heard Emma Hatton's terrible news regarding her sister's death.

It became the generally accepted theory that Frank Lamb had witnessed the spiritual body of Emily Frayne passing from this world to the next. Curiously, none of the neighbors, Frank Lamb included, ever put much stock in paranormal beliefs. Quite a few thought it odd that Frank Lamb would describe his mysterious visitor as a blonde-haired woman in a red floral dress while Emily Frayne had dark hair and was dressed in the black attire of a widow in mourning. Emma Hatton believed that Frank Lamb may have been experiencing a nightmare or may even have been in some sort of a dreamlike trance when he entered the hallway and learned of her sister's death. From this, she believed, his hallucination was born. It was also suggested that Lamb was occasionally known to sleepwalk.

In the days that followed, reports continued to circulate about the haunted building on Prospect. Some claimed that the tenants were continuing to witness the spectral manifestation of the ghostly woman, while others reported mysterious knocking sounds being heard throughout the building. It was even suggested that Emma Hatton's normally sedate clock struck its chime one hundred times. Spiritualistic mediums were said to have visited the room of Frank Lamb in hopes of conjuring the blonde woman, but no word was ever related of their success or failure in these endeavors.

The story of 54 Prospect Street being haunted by the ghost of Emily Frayne may sound familiar to some, as a slimmed-down version of this story has been covered once or twice in recent years, but what's been left out is what follows. This is the story that, until now, has been lost.

"The Ghost Shrieks." So declared the headline of an article that continued the story of the ghostly occurrences in January 1886.

Three days after the autopsy of Emily Frayne at the West Side Morgue, a local undertaker named William E. Heffron took charge of the remains and made arrangements to have the body returned to Ontario for burial. The body was picked up that Monday and conveyed to Heffron's facility at 212 Detroit Street, near the northwest corner of Detroit and Pearl. The undertaker was still in the process of building his new morgue and funeral parlor at that address; thus, the remains were placed in the deadhouse at the rear of the property. Next to the deadhouse were located the sleeping rooms for the employees and, beside them, a harness closet.

THE GHOST SHRIEKS.

Unearthly Sounds Heard About the Dead-House That Contained Mrs. Frayne's Body.

A Night of Terror Spent by Two Attendants of the Undertaking Establishment.

A headline reports on the ghostly activity at Heffron's undertaking parlor. *From the* Cleveland Leader, *1886.*

At around ten thirty that Wednesday evening, two of Heffron's employees, William Barker and Joseph Carr, were in the harness closet, smoking their pipes and polishing the harness plating. Suddenly, the two men were disturbed by pitiful cries, as if someone in the deadhouse was shrieking in great agony. They quickly ran to the front office and told Heffron that there was a sick woman in the makeshift morgue. Heffron dismissed this, as the place was locked and he possessed the only key. Barker persisted in his claim. To set the men at ease, Heffron went to the outbuilding and unlocked it. Emily Frayne's body lay before them, dead and silent as the grave. Heffron returned to the office and the other two to the harness closet. The men had been seated but a moment when the melancholy cries started up again. The sound had changed into a weird and unearthly moan. With blanched faces, the two frightened men returned to the front office but now refused to believe that the cries were those of a sick person. The room, they had plainly seen, contained only the remains of Emily Frayne, and their conclusion was just too terrible to be thought upon.

The Kendel Building occupies the site of Blair's Block. *Wikimedia Commons.*

Joseph Carr refused to sleep on-site and sought accommodations elsewhere. William Barker remained but refused to go near the deadhouse. Around midnight, William Heffron went to his room in the Adams House but awoke at four o'clock in the morning to Barker telling him that he'd no longer stay anywhere near the place. Barker was sent back but took a policeman with him. When Heffron returned an hour later, he found Barker in the office, still afraid to go anywhere near the back of the property. Both Carr and Barker later attested that neither had heard the story of what transpired at Blair's Block on Prospect, the circumstances surrounding the sudden death of Emily Frayne or what had unfolded in Frank Lamb's room at the moment of her death.

On Friday evening, the body of Emily Frayne was loaded onto a cart and delivered to the Union Depot. When the baggage master received the casket, he reviewed the paperwork. On seeing Emily Frayne's name, he recognized this as the body of the woman whose death had caused such a sensation on Prospect Street. He ordered it loaded onto one of the station baggage trucks but refused to stand anywhere near it. No one else would go anywhere near it either, as all seemed too afraid to risk a ghostly confrontation.

The casket was ultimately placed on a train, and Emily Frayne's body was returned to Hamilton, Ontario, where she was laid to rest in the family vault.

Blair's Block, which had been the scene of the initial haunting associated with the death of Emily Frayne, was demolished around 1915. The four-story Kendel Building at 210 Prospect Avenue, a beautiful example of Classical Revival architecture, was built on the site in 1918 and is now listed on the National Register of Historic Places. William E. Heffron's undertaking parlor on Detroit Street was only in use for a few years. By the mid-1890s, it housed a bowling alley and tailor's shop. The building was torn down around 1912 to accommodate an approach for the newly constructed Bulkley Boulevard. The southeast corner of a new office building at 2516 Detroit Avenue now stands on the former site of Heffron's undertaker's parlor, where the ghost of Emily Frayne was said to shriek.

CHAPTER 15

THE CLOSET DOOR
ON TAYLOR STREET

41.48142, -81.71827

She rose among us where we lay.
She wept, we put our work away.
She chilled our laughter, stilled our play;
And spread a silence there.
And darkness shot across the sky,
And once, and twice, we heard her cry;
And saw her lift white hands on high
And toss her troubled hair.
—*"The Vampire" by Conrad Aiken*

In mid-September 1887, occupation of a small frame house at the rear of 215 Taylor Street on Cleveland's West Side was taken up by James Donohue and his new bride. The front house was occupied by Theodore and Dora LaFrinier, who owned the property.

The bedroom of 215 Taylor Street Rear was located on the second floor of the little house. Off that bedroom was a small closet. After residing in the house for only two days, James Donohue awoke in the middle of the night and witnessed what he believed to be the ghostly image of the bust and torso of a woman appearing on the upstairs closet door. In her arms, the woman seemed to be cradling a sleeping infant. The image only appeared when the lights were turned down low. When they were completely extinguished, the image vanished entirely. Mrs. Donohue firmly believed the house to be haunted, though no strange or otherworldly noises were heard in connection with the apparition.

215 Taylor Street, circa 1961. *Courtesy the Cuyahoga County Archives.*

Over the next three nights, the Donohues witnessed the ghostly image returning. Finally, on September 20, the apparition of the woman and baby returned again, and the Donohues had reached the end of their tether. James Donohue contacted Patrolman Hibbard of the Cleveland Police Department, who came over to investigate the matter.

It was Hibbard's belief that the image was nothing more than a trick of the light or possibly even a case of white paint having been applied over a coat of dark paint. More than that, he believed that the image no more resembled a woman holding a baby than it did a spot on a closet door. He suggested that they simply paint the door.

The Donohues weren't buying it. They knew what they were seeing and vowed to move out of the house as soon as they could.

As far as the history of the house goes, it really isn't that interesting. Built around 1872, it was primarily used as a rental property. There was only one death reported in the place. That occurred on September 1, 1877, with the passing of ten-year-old Charles Henry Kay, a son of James H. Kay, who rented the house from 1873 through 1878. The boy's cause of death was diphtheria. The funeral was likely held at the home with the burial taking place in the family lot at Monroe Street Cemetery.

Curiously, on August 30, 1887, only two weeks before the Donahues moved into the house, Francis LaFrinier, Theodore and Dora's four-day-old child, passed away in the front house. Their ten-year-old son, Frank, had passed away there three years earlier.

It should be pointed out that this wasn't the first haunting of note reported along Taylor Street. In May 1880, the *West Side Sentinel* reported the appearance of a ghost along Taylor Street between Lorain and Ravine Streets to the south. It was said that the ghost appeared to several people but took on a different form each time. To one person, it appeared as "a shadowy light in the form of a woman," while another said it resembled something like a camel. This proved to be bad news for the neighborhood, as it attracted several young men, armed with shotguns, who hoped to meet the spectral being.

The house at 215 Taylor Street Rear ultimately carried the address 1910 West 45th Street. It was demolished in the 1980s and now exists as the empty backyard of the house at 1908 West 45th Street.

CHAPTER 16

PATROL STATION NO. 2 IS HAUNTED

41.49114, −81.71016

See that ol' barn jest over there that's so tipped-up an' canted,
That kinder tumble-down affair?—Wall, that ol' barn is han'ted.
That used to be Tom Phelan's barn, who died in eighty-seven,
Who tried his best for sixty years to fit himself for heaven.
—"Tom Phelan's Haunted Barn" by Sam Walter Foss

Policemen, as it was stated in September 1890, were not generally superstitious. Nevertheless, an officer on duty at Patrol Station No. 2 asserted that he didn't like to remain alone in the barn when the wagon was out. The reason? Ghosts.

The officer, who apparently wished to remain anonymous, stated that it was "the durnedest place to try and catch forty winks that I ever tilted a chair in." The whole thing started when the officer in question tried to take a nap while the wagon was out responding to a call. It was then that the telephone started ringing. He answered it, but there was no one on the line. This continued for some time. Finally, the officer placed the earpiece down so that the phone wouldn't ring, but sure enough, it started ringing again. He hung it back up, and for the next ten minutes, the phone continuously rang, this time to the tune of a song called "Little Annie Rooney."

The building that housed Patrol Station No. 2, according to the officer, belonged to the estate of an old citizen, who ended his career in affluence and now slept under a big monument at Riverside Cemetery. It was a large, two-story brick barn that had once housed some remarkable horses—not to

A Cleveland police wagon, circa late 1800s. *Cleveland State University. Michael Schwartz Library.*

say that John and Ike, the two horses that pulled the patrol wagon, were any less magnificent. Set on Vermont Street at the northwest corner where it met Hanover, which later became West 28th Street, the station resembled a fire engine house more than anything else. The facility was leased in 1886 by the police department for a term of five years at a rate of $200 per year. The property was part of the estate of the late Elias Sims, whose house sat just to the north at the corner of Hanover and Washington Streets.

Captain Elias Sims, a son of John and Eliza Sims of Onondaga County, New York, was born in that place on August 4, 1813. At the age of fifteen, he went to work as a mule driver on the Erie Canal, and three years later, he took a job as a contractor on that waterway. In 1838, he was married to Cornelia Vosburgh, with whom he had four children. In the years that followed, he went to work in Canada and operated a dredger. He then came to Cleveland in 1855 to dredge the Old Riverbed. In time, he built a fortune in dredging and in the construction of the Great Western Railroad in Canada. In 1867, he established the Rocky River Railroad, which started at present-day West 58th Street and Bridge Avenue and ended at the west end of Lakewood. Elias Sims died on Sunday, April 5, 1885, at his farm near Parma. The funeral was held at his home on Washington and Hanover two days later.

Elias Sims. *From* History of Cuyahoga County, Ohio, *1879.*

Relating further stories of the haunted barn, the anonymous police officer claimed that the back doors would fly open with a bang. No sooner would he close them than the front door would open, then close and lock itself again. It was also stated that the officers frequently heard the sound of footsteps in the loft above. These came almost every night from dark to sunrise. Sometimes they were so quiet that they were barely audible. Other times they sounded as loud as someone dancing in wooden shoes. When they were that loud, it would set the horses on edge, sometimes to the point that they broke their halters and trembled with fright. Most of the officers were, by this point, so used to it that it no longer bothered them. Still, it would take some time to break in a new man.

It was also claimed that the patrol house was haunted by a ghostly tomcat. At first, the officers tried to chase it off by throwing things at it, but these items passed right through it. They then tried shooting it, but this also proved ineffective.

In all honesty, there really was nothing nefarious in the history of the barn itself. The only recorded incident of interest to have occurred there was the theft of a clothes wringer and several other articles in August 1875. The nearby Sims house, on the other hand, saw quite a few deaths.

Charles R. Evatt, Elias Sims's forty-one-year-old son-in-law, passed away at that residence in October 1874. November 27, 1876, saw the passing of Cornelia Vosburgh Sims. The Simses' nine-year-old grandson, Elias Sims Evatt, died at the home just three weeks later from convulsions. Their granddaughter, Olivia Starkweather, died there on July 13, 1884.

Contrary to the officer's claim that Sims was taking his repose beneath a large monument at Riverside, he was, in fact, entombed at nearby Monroe Street Cemetery. The Sims family vault was built in 1868 to receive the remains of Sims's daughter, Sarah Jane Evatt, who died the previous May. All other members of that family were afterward likewise entombed there.

In 1924, Elias and Cornelia's daughter, Leafie Sims Starkweather, passed away and was buried at Lake View Cemetery beside her husband, who'd died in 1899. On June 12, 1931, their son, William J. Starkweather, had the

The site of Patrol Station No. 2 today. *Photo by William G. Krejci.*

remains of his sister Olivia, and those of his grandparents, removed from the family vault at Monroe and reinterred at Lake View. Three months later, he ordered the remains of Charles, Sarah and Elias Evatt removed from the vault and reburied immediately to the north of it. The reason for this was never explained. Now empty, the vault is used by the Monroe Street Cemetery Foundation for the storage of gardening tools and flags that are placed seasonally on veterans' graves.

In 1892, a new West Side police station was built, and Patrol Station No. 2 was moved to that new facility at the corner of State and Church Streets. Like William Heffron's funeral parlor of the previous chapter, the Elias Sims House, as well as the barn that for five years carried the reputation of being a haunted police station, were demolished to make way for Bulkley Boulevard.

CHAPTER 17
THE LIEBENGOOD GHOST

41.50035, -81.68481

"A Jolly Place," said he, "in times of old!
But something ails it now: the spot is curst."
—"Hart-Leap Well" by William Wordsworth

Euclid Avenue, according to Mark Twain, was one of the finest streets in America. He also observed that the dwellings were very large and often pretty pretentious architecturally. One can only wonder what his comments would have been had he learned that one of those dwellings was said to be haunted.

Pennsylvania native Charles Liebengood, a yardmaster for the Nickel Plate Railroad, moved into the two-story frame house at 479 Euclid Avenue with his wife, Sarah Ann, and their five children in March 1892. That first year was quiet, but the following summer was a different situation altogether.

The first to witness the ghostly manifestation was Anna Hogan, Mr. and Mrs. Liebengood's niece, who briefly resided with them. It was sometime in the middle of the night when Anna awoke to see a woman, dressed in a long white robe that trailed to the ground, standing at the foot of her bed. In her hand, the strange visitor carried a book. At first, Anna thought that it was her aunt and asked her why she was up at that hour. When the woman didn't reply, Anna realized that it wasn't her aunt at all and screamed. This awakened Sarah Ann Liebengood, but before she could find out where the noise had originated, her niece came running breathlessly into the bedroom and related what she'd witnessed. The Liebengoods attributed her experience to an overactive imagination and sent her back to bed.

The following night, one of the Liebengoods' sons was stricken with a severe toothache. Charles stayed with the boy in the same bedroom where Anna Hogan had experienced the uncanny visitor. Apparently, she'd refused to continue to occupy that room. Charles Liebengood was sleeping with his back to the wall when he received a sudden blow to the face, as though someone had slapped him with an open hand. He looked up to see the ghost of the woman standing over him. At first, he thought it was his sister, Sallie, but then a sliver of light shone in through the window. It touched the face of the phantom, revealing it in all of its ghastliness. Charles Liebengood grabbed his son and quickly carried the boy from the room. When his wife found him, he could hardly talk.

The phantasm continued to appear to the Liebengood family throughout the rest of the summer and well into late September. On one occasion, Sarah Ann Liebengood recalled, the spectral woman was standing at the foot of her bed. She was holding a book in her outstretched hand. Before Sarah Ann Liebengood could crawl out of bed, the ghost grabbed her by the leg, but it released her a moment later. The same had happened to Charles Liebengood. When the ghost seized him, however, he found his leg paralyzed.

That October, the family went public with the happenings at their home on Euclid Avenue. It was said that the white-draped ghostly female glided mysteriously about the place, slamming doors and tweaking the noses of the family as they slept. During the day, the family could plainly hear the woman walking about the haunted room and up and down the stairway. At night, the children refused to go to bed unless accompanied by one of their parents and a light. The Liebengoods made it clear that they'd had enough. They moved out of the house on October 3, 1893, and took up residency at a home on Shafer Court. Eventually, they moved back to Pennsylvania.

A neighbor who lived across the alley behind the haunted house also claimed to have seen the ghost late one afternoon. The story was creating quite a stir in the neighborhood, and wild tales began to circulate. Some even put it about that a terrible crime had once been committed in the house. That claim was debunked by Henry Lee Cross, who lived in the massive brick mansion immediately to the east at 483 Euclid Avenue. Cross, as it turned out, was the owner of the haunted house and was born there in 1851. The house was built in the 1830s by his maternal grandfather, Major Seth Lafayette Lee, and later passed into the hands of his parents, David and Loraine Cross. The Cross family continued to occupy it until building the large brick house that they currently occupied. After moving into their

UNEASY SPIRIT.

A Ghost Said to Haunt a Euclid Avenue ~ House.

The Tenant is Badly Worried.

Right: A headline announces the haunting at the Liebengood home. *From the* Plain Dealer, *1893.*

Below: The Liebengood home appears immediately to the right of the Cross House, which is identifiable by the large tower. *Photo courtesy Cleveland Public Library Photograph Collection.*

new home, they leased the original to their nephew, Isaac Newton. The Liebengoods were only the fifth occupants, and according to Henry Cross, no terrible crime had ever been committed there.

Cross claimed that the ghost was easily explained away. Charles Liebengood had been seeking a reduction in his rent but was refused. Ultimately, Henry Cross agreed to let him simply move out. This explanation was generally accepted by the public, and the Liebengood Ghost on Euclid Avenue was soon forgotten.

The alleged haunted house was torn down just a few years later to make way for a commercial block that was relatively short-lived. It was replaced in 1911 by the fifteen-story Cleveland Athletic Club Building. Today, that structure exists as the Athlon Building and houses 163 luxury suite apartments.

CHAPTER 18

COMMERCIAL STREET

41.49223, −81.68556

The ghost appeared only once, and it went by very dim to the sight and floated
noiseless through the air, and then disappeared.
—The Mysterious Stranger *by Mark Twain*

The night of August 27, 1897, was a restless one for those who resided in the area of Commercial Street, on the hillside above the east bank of the Cuyahoga River. Another Cleveland ghost story was about to unfold.

It was just around nine thirty when Mrs. John Schaefer, who lived at 12 Berg Street, just east of Commercial Street, looked across the road and noticed a strange and curious figure slowly drifting down the avenue opposite where she stood. In her realization of what she was witnessing, she nearly fainted away. It was a large fireball, the color of burnished gold, that kept changing its shape. Finally, it was plainly identifiable as the disembodied head of a woman. The lady's face was dark but phosphorescent and constantly changed color. It was said that her face was convulsed as though she were in some terrible agony and that an abundance of dark and waving hair fluttered out around her head, which at times hid the grotesque expression on her face.

As soon as Mrs. Schaefer was able to catch her breath and compose herself, she let out a loud scream and fled toward her house. This roused others in the neighborhood, and they ran to the scene, where they were confronted by the same manifestation that Mrs. Schaefer had witnessed. In a matter of

Above: A view along Commercial Street looking southeast down Berg, circa 1920. *Cleveland State University. Michael Schwartz Library.*

Left: Commercial Road today. *Photo by William G. Krejci.*

moments, a large crowd had gathered. Others, seeing the assemblage and thinking it a brawl, came running over with curiosity. They, too, were met with the phantom head.

Witnesses said that the head flitted back and forth and rolled and careened about in a startling manner. It grew in size and fearfulness, and the nerves of some of those present were overcome by the terror before them. The police were notified of the disturbance, and a small detachment was ordered to the scene. Sergeant Doering, in the company of Patrolmen Stanton, Gill and Lyle, could hear the melee over a block away. They arrived and eventually succeeded, after much difficulty, in dispersing the crowd. They then turned their attention to figuring out the cause of the phenomenon.

It was supposed that the phantom image was actually caused by the headlamp of a streetcar crossing the nearby Central Avenue Viaduct. The officers believed the light was reflecting off storefront windows. This, however, didn't account for the ghost's appearance when there were no streetcars crossing the viaduct. The mystery was never solved.

Within a couple of hours, the manifestation disappeared entirely. Neighbors hung around late into the night, puzzling over what they had seen and discussing the matter with bated breath.

Curiously, this appearance occurred roughly one thousand feet from the site of the storied House on the Commons that appears in chapter 1. Eventually, the neighborhood was leveled, and the area gave way to progress. All the streets have been erased entirely, save one. Commercial Road, as it's now called, has been rerouted from its original course and descent into the flats. That's really all that remains to show that this neighborhood ever existed. Most of the site is now a parking lot and an overgrown hillside.

CHAPTER 19

THE COTTAGE ON NINE MILE CREEK

41.54256, -81.55447

And travellers, now, within that valley,
Through the red-litten windows see
Vast forms that move fantastically
To a discordant melody;
While, like a ghastly rapid river,
Through the pale door
A hideous throng rush out forever,
And laugh—but smile no more.
—"The Haunted Palace" by Edgar Allan Poe

It was said that, in its day, the deep gully of Nine Mile Creek, near Collamer Village, was a paradise for hunters. Thickly wooded and dense with undergrowth, its narrow, winding paths traversed the steep embankments and crossed the ravine in many places. Carefully hidden among the tall hemlocks of that vale was a small hillside cottage that was whispered, among those few who knew of its existence, to be haunted. Difficult to reach, it would only be found accidentally by hunters in that sylvan glen.

Such was the case in the fall of 1898 when two Cleveland policemen, Sergeant John W. Anderson Jr. and Patrolman Kinsey Fife of the Sixth Precinct, were hunting on the land of their friend Dr. George F. Leick, who owned an estate of fifty acres that fronted nearby Euclid Avenue. It was only by happenstance that the two stumbled upon the cottage. After returning to Dr. Leick's house that evening, the men made an inquiry regarding the strange little house in the adjacent woods. It was explained that the house sat on property that had belonging to Dr. Leick's former neighbor, the late Josephine Ammon.

Born Josephine Mary Saxton, she entered the world on January 3, 1844, in Cassopolis, Michigan. At the age of seven, she relocated with her parents, Jehiel and Emeline, to Cleveland, where she'd spend the rest of her life. By the age of fourteen, she was working as a schoolteacher, though she would also devote herself to spiritualistic and charitable work as a humanitarian, often assisting the city's poor.

On January 9, 1863, she was married to Colonel John Henry Ammon, with whom she'd raise four children. Not long after taking their nuptials, the couple purchased a large tract of land near Collamer Village, but also kept a house in Cleveland. Both homes were located on the illustrious Euclid Avenue. Josephine's marriage to Colonel Ammon lasted just under twenty-five years. On November 30, 1887, she was granted a divorce on the grounds of abandonment.

In the absence of her husband in the months leading up to the termination of her marriage, Josephine Ammon was joined in her home by a wealthy widow named Persis Blann and the widow's forty-five-year-old unwed daughter, Josie.

On December 26, 1887, Persis Blann died from dropsy at the Ammon home and was interred a few days later at Lake View Cemetery. Following

The Ammon Farm near Collamer Village. *From* Atlas of Cuyahoga County, Ohio, *1874.*

the funeral, a great controversy arose regarding Persis Blann's estate, the majority of which was willed to Josie. It was claimed that Josie Blann was of a diminished mental capacity, and a guardian was appointed by a judge to handle her estate. Believing the guardian desired to have his ward committed to an asylum, Josie went into hiding. When her court-appointed guardian, an attorney named Johnson, arrived at the Ammon home, he was refused admittance. The police were called, and a search of both of Josephine Ammon's properties was made. A few days later, Josephine Ammon was called into court but refused to divulge Josie Blann's location. In regard to where the woman was, Ammon stated that she didn't know but had an idea. At this, she was found in contempt of court and was remanded to the county jail. She later boasted that she was the first woman ever to be sent to jail for having an idea.

The case made national headlines, and Josephine Ammon was visited by a constant stream of friends and admirers. Within a few days, her entire jail cell was fitted up with artwork and comfortable furnishings from her home. After forty-one days of incarceration, Josephine Ammon decided to come clean. She explained to the judge that on December 31, 1887, Josie Blann had come to her and requested to be taken by carriage to a farm in Bainbridge. Since that time, she'd not heard from her. At this, the judge dropped the charge of contempt and had her released.

When Josephine returned to her home, she had her parlor fitted up in the same manner that her cell had been. It was then that she decided to seek a retreat from her mansion and even her country estate near Collamer and had the cottage on Nine Mile Creek erected.

Dr. George Leick described Josephine Ammon's haunted house, stating that a visit to the mysterious structure was well worth the trouble met with in reaching it. It was not easily found, as it was quite well hidden among the tall hemlocks. Standing on the eastern slope of a steep incline, it was approached by a series of small, winding paths. Suddenly, visitors would find themselves at an arched bridge. Passing over this bridge brought them onto the roof of the house, where a cupola was placed for the accommodation of pigeons and other birds. At the edge of the roof, a winding stairway led down to the entrance of the house. Other stairways led down the slope of the ravine.

On entering the house, visitors found that it consisted of only three rooms. One of these was a parlor. Growing from the floor of that room was a massive tree, which passed through the roof of the house. The entire affair was richly furnished, and the interior walls were covered with valuable

Josephine Ammon's jail cell. *Photo courtesy Western Reserve Historical Society.*

paintings and etchings by Otto Henry Bacher. It was also said that not a single nail was used in the construction of the cottage and that it was secure and staunch, the workmanship that went into building it having been of the highest quality.

Far below the cottage ran the rapid waters of Nine Mile Creek. Nearly as far above was the top of the ravine's bank. It was in this isolated woodland cottage that Josephine Ammon spent a year in reflection and solitude.

In due time, death comes for everyone, some sooner than others. In the early morning hours of Sunday, June 5, 1892, death called on Josephine Mary Ammon at her lavish Euclid Avenue home in Cleveland. She was forty-eight. Surrounded by her family and friends, she departed with the words, "Be good and kind to the poor and unfortunate, for the rich can take care of themselves." She was laid to rest at Lake View Cemetery in a quiet spot she'd selected, southeast of President Garfield's monument.

At her funeral, Josephine Ammon was eulogized by Hudson P. Tuttle, an eminent spiritualist from Berlin Heights. He spoke at length on the great deeds of charity carried out by his friend in her lifetime but concluded with a cryptic notion. He stated that Josephine had not died but had simply been translated to a higher sphere and higher work, from which she would often return to care for her parents and children. "For," he said, "we not only believe in life beyond the grave, but the power to return here. Life would be dreary indeed were that not so, and can you imagine a place so sweet that the spirit would not want to return to its loved ones, and not to feel that she had gone but still had a presence over them."

It was soon after Josephine's death that the little cottage on Nine Mile Creek gained the reputation of being haunted. Though no specifics of paranormal events were ever related, Hudson Tuttle's graveside words may have inspired the notion.

Three months after the death of Josephine Ammon, a man named George Davies, who worked as a commission merchant in Cleveland, was involved in a financial embarrassment. He disappeared for almost a year, and his whereabouts had always been something of a mystery. In telling the story of the haunted house on Nine Mile Creek, Dr. Leick finally solved that mystery by disclosing the fact that Davies had holed up at the deserted cottage and lived there entirely by himself. Sadly, Davies was murdered by his wife, Hannah, on February 9, 1897. Following an argument that

Site of the cottage on Nine Mile Creek today. *Photo by William G. Krejci.*

morning at the breakfast table, she withdrew to her bedroom, returned with a pistol and shot him in the head.

By the late 1890s, the rich etchings and paintings that once adorned the walls of the cottage had disappeared entirely. It was suggested that they were stolen by tramps, but Dr. Leick intimated that tramps had no use for such items and that they were likely stolen by vandals who knew their worth.

Today, much of Nine Mile Creek in that area has been rerouted through a culvert. Belvoir Boulevard now runs along the bottom of the ravine. The site of the cottage is just inside of Cleveland Heights, near its border with East Cleveland. Its exact location was on a small terrace, halfway up the hillside, on the east side of Quilliams Creek and southeast of its confluence at Nine Mile Creek. This terrace sits about 350 feet southeast of Belvoir Boulevard. Not a single trace of the haunted house on Nine Mile Creek remains.

CHAPTER 20

THE MALDEN STREET SPOOK

41.52382, -81.63451

Some people do not believe in ghosts.
For that matter, some people do not believe in anything.
—The Open Door *by Charlotte Riddell*

Achieving the American dream can mean so many different things to so many different people. Some see it as sharing in the opportunities afforded every American. For others, it's maintaining a home filled with tranquility and bliss. Sadly, that tranquility can be upset by the smallest of things, such as an unexpected visitor from a ghostly realm.

The site of this next haunting was a solid two-story wooden house, built around 1890, that originally carried the address 55 Malden Street. Within a few short years, the address was changed to 225 Malden. It was while carrying that address that it gained its notoriety. The home was purchased by German immigrants John and Mary Schultz in February 1895 for $1,300. The couple promptly moved in with their five children.

For a little over five years, the Schultzes enjoyed their little piece of the American dream, but that all changed on the afternoon of Monday, June 11, 1900.

At about two thirty, Mary Schultz was getting her son Herman's dinner ready. Herman, who worked at a wire mill, had just gotten up and was getting ready for work. His fifteen-year-old sister, Mary, was in the kitchen, while his mother was looking out the back door. Suddenly, they all heard a loud crashing noise in the parlor. When they went to investigate, they found a picture of the Last Supper lying on the floor with the glass broken. The cord on the back was still intact, and the hook from which it had hung was not bent. Mary Schultz thought little of this. She rehung the picture and closed the parlor door but returned an hour later to find several more pictures lying on the floor and leaning against the wall. Not one of them was broken or scratched. At first, she blamed her younger children and securely fastened the windows and the door to keep them out.

Beginning at seven o'clock the following morning, Mary Schultz found bric-a-brac, a number of knickknacks and several more pictures on the floor, though nothing was broken. She promptly rehung the pictures but closely watched the parlor for three hours. Nothing occurred. A few neighbors agreed to watch the front of the house to make sure that no one was entering the room through a window. Mary Schultz locked the parlor door again. She returned twenty minutes later and found the pictures again knocked to the floor, yet not a soul had been seen entering the room. This went on about ten times that day.

Wednesday and Thursday transpired in much the same manner. Some neighbors insisted on rehanging the pictures themselves, believing that they wouldn't come down if hung by someone outside of the family, but the result was the same.

In relating the story of what had been transpiring in her home, Mary Schultz claimed that her eleven-year-old daughter, Emma, suffered from a weakness. She stated that an Indian herbalist had recently treated her but now alleged that a bewitchment of some sort was affecting the girl. Some of the more superstitious neighbors suggested that Mary Schultz remove from her home an ornamental sheaf of wheat that they believed to be enchanted. The item had been placed on Mary Schultz's father's casket at his funeral some six months earlier. Those same neighbors suggested that she exhume the remains of her father to see if he'd turned in his coffin. This, they said, would indicate that he'd been buried alive. Mary Schultz flatly refused to do this, stating that her father, a man named Rehburg who died in South Euclid at the age of seventy-seven, was quite dead when he was buried.

On Friday morning, Emma Schultz came running to her mother in terror. She claimed that a framed printed motto that hung above the parlor door slowly slid down the wall to the floor. The motto read: "I Need Thee Every Hour." Mary Schultz ushered everyone away from the room and locked it up again. When she returned to it later, she found flowers that had been placed in vases now strewn about the room. One of the vases

SPOOKS IN DAYLIGHT.

Malden Street Excited Over Peculiar Happenings.

HOUSE OF THE SCHULTZES.

PICTURES DROP FROM THE WALLS OR SLOWLY DESCEND.

A headline reports on the strange happenings in the home of the Schwartz family. *From the Cleveland Leader, 1900.*

had been smashed. A peculiar odor was also said to permeate the parlor, adding to the terror of the situation.

Curiously, and unlike most other reported hauntings, the ghost never seemed to make its presence known at night. In fact, ghostly activity in the Schultz home was never witnessed any later than four o'clock in the afternoon.

Word spread rapidly through the neighborhood of what was going on at the Schultz home, and by Friday afternoon, a crowd of nearly two hundred people had converged on Malden Street. That evening, a neighbor named Louis Howald called on the Schultzes and asked if they would agree to permit a city official to go through the house and make a search for the mysterious spook, to which they consented, though no ghost was found. That night, more neighbors arrived, quite indignant over the situation, and threatened the Schultzes that if the stories of the haunting didn't cease, the police would be called in to deal with the matter.

On Saturday morning, Howald returned again, this time with a man the Schultzes didn't know, and again asked to be let in. They refused him entry and sent him away. Shortly after, a patrolman named Grimes arrived and noticed that the blinds and shutters of the haunted parlor were drawn and closed. He ordered them opened so as to permit anyone who happened to be passing outside a glimpse of the ghost at its work. They complied, but when the patrolman returned later that afternoon, he found the curtains and shutters once again closed.

A number of newspaper reporters called on the Schultzes that afternoon but were promptly sent away, being informed that the ghost had not returned. One reporter pressed the matter, and John Schultz finally explained that he was infuriated by the fact that one newspaper had insinuated that his eleven-year-old daughter was behind the mischief. This, he claimed, was impossible, as there was not a single chair in the entire house tall enough for her to stand on to reach the pictures.

It might also be suggested that the threats of the indignant neighbors likewise had a bearing on the haunting coming to its sudden end. Whether the paranormal activity had actually ceased remains a mystery. Perhaps it was just better to deal with it and remain silent.

Sometimes the history of a house can speak volumes, especially when relating to ghostly activity; however, a look at this house's past reveals very little. In 1900, when the story of the haunting emerged, the house was only about ten years old. What's more, the only known death to have occurred there was when a four-month-old boy named William, a son of the original owners, John and Wilhelmina Schimmelmann, died of convulsions in early January 1894.

Things remained quiet at 225 Malden Street, but just two years after the haunting took place, John Schultz passed away in the home and was buried at Woodland Cemetery. In 1906, the address was changed to 1143 East 78th Street. It stayed in the Schultz family until Mary's passing in the late 1920s.

225 Malden Street, circa 1959. *Courtesy the Cuyahoga County Archives.*

By 1973, the house had fallen into disrepair, but that January, it was undergoing a renovation. A guard dog was tied up in the empty house, chained to a gas heater. The dog, it was believed, pulled the heater from the wall and started a fire, causing $3,000 in damage. The dog and house were both saved, and the house was still standing in the early 1980s, but it has since been torn down. Today, the site of 225 Malden is occupied by a grassy empty lot.

CHAPTER 21
GRACE EPISCOPAL CHURCH

41.49875, -81.68579

Now is the time of night
That the graves all gaping wide,
Every one lets forth his sprite
In the church-way paths to glide.
—A Midsummer Night's Dream *by William Shakespeare*

While popularly haunted in British lore, churches in the United States are not generally thought to be places where ghosts are said to linger. Some are of the belief that God would never allow such an intrusion in a holy house of worship. But what of a church that's slated for demolition? Are ghosts permitted to haunt those unconsecrated structures during their final days?

In the spring of 1902, demolition was the sad fate in store for Grace Episcopal Church, which was located at the southwest corner of Huron Road and East 9th Street, then still called Erie Street. The parish that occupied the Gothic Revival structure was established on July 9, 1845. The cornerstone for their church was laid on September 28, 1846, and the first service was held on Easter Sunday 1848. More recently, the congregation had steadily drifted eastward on account of the ever-expanding business district of downtown Cleveland. The final service was held on May 25, 1902. It was at that time that the consecration of the building was removed by the bishop.

A few weeks later, demolition of the building commenced and was handled by a crew of men set to the task of dismantling the building and clearing the

Grace Episcopal Church, circa 1874. *Photo courtesy Cleveland Public Library Photograph Collection.*

debris by hand. On the afternoon of Thursday, September 11, as a number of men were engaged in the work, a well-dressed woman picked her way over the debris and inquired about the location of a coffin she claimed had been buried beneath the chancel. The foreman wasn't present, so they had no answers for her.

After she left, the men found that they couldn't continue the work. The mere thought that they had been throwing bricks down on a dead man's head filled them with terror, for surely, the place must be haunted. Henry Ross, who'd been assigned to knock down a wall, firmly believed that one of the men would surely be killed on that job for piling up debris on a grave site. When the foreman returned, he ordered the men back to work, but they flatly refused and almost walked off the job. He pleaded with them and urged them to be brave, stating that ghosts were never seen in daylight. Apparently, the events of Malden Street two years earlier had slipped his mind. Slowly, the men returned to work, but not one of them would venture anywhere near the rear of the building where the coffin was said to be located. It was reported that some of the men never returned to the jobsite for fear of the otherworldly beings that might haunt the location.

One who did return that Saturday was George Williams. Arriving around six o'clock that morning, while it was still dark out and before anyone else showed up, Williams grabbed a pick, crowbar and shovel and descended into the basement beneath the chancel. According to Williams, when he reached the crypt, he peered into the inky blackness, and before him there advanced an object darker than the surrounding space. Slowly and majestically it moved, and with it came a cold, clammy breeze. The specter, he said, wore a millinery creation, composed of a black cloth, and the rest of the figure was robed in the same somber hue.

At seeing the manifestation, George Williams dropped his tools, screamed and fled in terror. He didn't stop until reaching the YMCA building on the other side of the street. It was there that he was met by his friend Sol Cephus, who was just arriving for work. The foreman saw them across the street and inquired why they weren't at work. Rather than admit that he was frightened, George Williams turned to his friend, saying that the sound of him dropping his tools probably scared off the ghost anyway, and with that, the two men returned to the jobsite.

As it turns out, there wasn't one coffin buried beneath Grace Episcopal Church, but rather two.

Timothy Jarvis Carter was born in 1825 in New Rochelle, New York, a son of Mary Ann and Reverend Lawson Carter. Following in his father's footsteps, he entered the ministry and first served at Calvary Church in New York City. He left to become the rector of Cleveland's newly built Grace Episcopal Church in November 1849.

Reverend Carter hadn't been serving long as rector when he suddenly took ill. It was around that time that he made the acquaintance of Emma

Cornelia Clark Woolson, a daughter of Hannah and Charles Woolson. Her friends described her fondly as a very beautiful girl and so full of life. When Emma realized that Reverend Carter wouldn't recover from his illness, she agreed to marry him, and the two traveled to Avon Springs, New York, where they were wed by Reverend Carter's father on May 7, 1851. They resided at 110 Ninth Street in New York City, where Emma nursed her husband through his illness and stayed with him to the end. He died there on November 15, 1851, from Bright's disease. Reverend Timothy Jarvis Carter was twenty-six.

Emma, whom some believed had lost her will to live, contracted tuberculosis and joined her husband in death on August 14, 1852. She was nineteen. It having been Reverend Carter's desire that his remains be deposited beneath the chancel where he'd performed his pastoral duty in breaking the bread of life for his flock, his wishes were complied with, and his interment took place on Saturday, November 22, 1851. His widow's remains were interred beside him two days after her passing the following year.

Edward Worthington, rector of Grace Episcopal Church at the time of its closing and demolition, explained that the caskets of Reverend Carter and his wife were removed from the church earlier that spring. They were

Opposite: Demolition of Grace Episcopal Church, circa 1902. *Photo courtesy Western Reserve Historical Society.*

Above: This white slab marks the burial site of Reverend Timothy and Emma Carter at Woodland Cemetery. *Photo by William G. Krejci.*

laid to rest together on May 28, 1902, in lot 2, section 5 of Woodland Cemetery and are buried beside the reverend's father, who succeeded him as rector of Grace Church after his passing. Their grave is marked by a flat white slab.

Following the demolition of Grace Episcopal Church, a one-story brick commercial block was put up on the site. That structure was replaced in 1925 by the three-story Huron Ninth Building.

CHAPTER 22

ADAMS STREET CEMETERY

41.36376, -81.84848

*I cannot tell what sentiment haunted the quiet solitary churchyard with its
inscribed headstone; its gate, its two trees, its low horizon, girdled by a broken
wall, and its newly-risen crescent, attesting the hour of even-tide.*
—Jane Eyre *by Charlotte Brontë*

While churches in the United States aren't commonly thought of as
being haunted, churchyards and cemeteries are an entirely different
matter altogether. American folklore is dotted with spooky tales of
grisly phantasms drifting among the headstones. Many such reported burial
grounds can readily be found in northern Ohio. Among them is the Adams
Street Cemetery in Berea. With stories of this cemetery dating back decades,
no one is certain where or when the ghostly legends originated. That mystery
has finally been solved.

Adams Street Cemetery rests in a tranquil part of town, adjoining the
western end of a residential area that sees little traffic. Aside from the few
nearby houses and American Legion Post 91, located immediately to the
south, the serenity of that burial ground is accented by woods and picturesque
Coe Lake. An Ohio historical marker placed near the cemetery's entrance
explains that it was established in 1834 and that it was originally known as
the Village Cemetery.

Many of the area's earliest pioneering families are laid to rest there, as are
numerous veterans, mayors and civic leaders. Also listed among those who
take their repose at Adams Street is Rosa Colvin, who died at the hands of
Alexander McConnell in 1866, mentioned in chapter 3.

On February 17, 1874, the Cuyahoga Stone Company purchased from the Village of Berea the land adjoining Adams Street Cemetery and commenced quarrying the rich sandstone from the earth. Unfortunately, the company brought its operations too close to the cemetery grounds and, over time, caused considerable flooding in the area. This also resulted in a significant landslide in the northwest corner of the graveyard, which toppled headstones and uncovered at least one coffin. At this, a number of graves were relocated to other nearby cemeteries that seemed safer places to inter the dead. Among those moved were five veterans of the Civil War. A few other families, whose loved ones' graves were not affected by the landslide, erred on the side of caution and followed suit.

Some suspected that the disturbance of these graves may have been what led to the haunting in the first place. Here's how the events unfolded.

In the fall of 1902, as someone was strolling past the cemetery after nightfall, they witnessed what appeared to be a pale, flickering halo playing about the monument erected to the unknown dead of the Civil War, which was later rededicated as a veterans' memorial. Within a few days, the spectacle was seen by a number of other people, but it always took on a different form. To some, it appeared as a sheeted ghost, while others witnessed a phantom head. No two people could agree on the aspect of the figure, only that it was of supernatural origin.

Some dared to approach it, but as they did so, the phantom floated over to the edge of a seventy-five-foot precipice to the north, then drifted out over the open chasm of the quarry. It was believed by some area residents to be the restless spirit of the person whose grave was exposed in the recent landslide.

One unnamed witness to the paranormal events at Adams Street Cemetery stated: "I never believed in ghosts before, but this certainly looks queer. We saw a pale, flickering light moving about among the gravestones. I should have thought it was a lantern, but the light was too ghastly for that. We watched the thing until it came to the edge of the graveyard by the bluff. There it seemed to hesitate for a minute, right where that old grave used to be, and then it floated off into the air and disappeared."

Some suggested that the phenomenon was caused by ignited swamp gas, but the terrain and soil conditions weren't favorable, as no marshes existed in the area. Also, the ghostly light was seen to pass through solid objects, such as stone walls and fences. Some neighbors feared that it might come into their homes and make away with them. During the day, most would pass the cemetery only if they had to, and even then would do so in haste, with sidelong glances. Hardly a soul dared to do so at night.

The northwest corner of Adams Street Cemetery overlooking Coe Lake. *Photo by William G. Krejci.*

In time, a number of tenants living in the vicinity of the Adams Street Cemetery started to move away. They gave different excuses for their desire to depart, but the landlords were certain that it was in response to the cemetery ghost. Houses sat empty, and landlords were in need of a solution.

That solution was found in the hiring of a thirty-five-year-old detective from Cleveland named Jake Mintz. On the night of Saturday, November 15, 1902, Mintz sent one of his hired assistants to Berea to keep an eye on the cemetery, but no ghostly activity was observed. The same was true the following night.

That Monday, an article appeared in the *Plain Dealer* regarding the haunting at Adams Street Cemetery. Coincidentally, Mintz received a call that same evening from his assistant in Berea, stating that the ghost had returned. Mintz immediately grabbed his revolvers, boarded a streetcar and arrived at the graveyard, where he met with his hired man shortly before midnight. Why he didn't ask this assistant to go into the cemetery and first investigate the matter before making the one-hour trolley ride to Berea is anyone's guess.

According to Mintz, he and his assistant observed the cemetery for some time but didn't see anything amiss. He was about to call it a night and return home to Cleveland when, suddenly, the white figure appeared. It seemed to be moving from one monument to another. Without taking any apparent consideration that this might be a person wearing a sheet, Mintz raised one of his revolvers and fired. Though he struck the figure, his shot had no effect. He then unloaded both of his revolvers at the figure, while his assistant completely emptied one of his. Still, the phantom lingered. Jake Mintz borrowed his assistant's remaining loaded weapon and charged at the figure, firing until every chamber was empty. He then dove and tackled the ghost, which turned out to be a sheet attached to two hundred feet of string.

The following day, Mintz spoke to reporters on the matter, and in pointing out the numerous holes in the sheet, bragged somewhat of his skills as a marksman. One has to wonder: was all of this an elaborate hoax, as Mintz claimed, or was it simply the answer that desperate landlords were looking for? Either way, it seemed to do the trick. There was little talk afterward regarding Adams Street Cemetery being haunted.

The cemetery continued receiving burials well into the twentieth century, but those were mainly indigents and paupers. Most interments were taking

Volunteers repair damage at Berea's Adams Street Cemetery. *Berea Historical Society*.

place at nearby Woodvale Cemetery. In time, the little cemetery on Adams Street had fallen into a severe state of neglect.

In March 1930, and again on Halloween night 1953, Adams Street Cemetery was the victim of terrible acts of vandalism and desecration. Many headstones and monuments, some so old that their epitaphs were almost completely illegible, were knocked over and shattered.

In the days that followed, American Legion Post 91 repaired those stones and continues to care for and decorate the graves of veterans. In recent years, the cemetery has been restored through the assistance of many community groups and the City of Berea. Students and faculty at nearby Baldwin Wallace University have documented the burials and continue to volunteer their time repairing damaged headstones.

CHAPTER 23

The Horace Street Haunting

41.47903, -81.70879

It was shrouded in a deep black garment, which concealed its head, its face, its form, and left nothing of it visible save one outstretched hand. But for this it would have been difficult to detach its figure from the night, and separate it from the darkness by which it was surrounded.
—A Christmas Carol *by Charles Dickens*

Charles Burchart arrived in Cleveland in 1902 with his wife and two of their children. In all, they had four, but the other two were staying with family in the West. In a short time, Burchart found employment as an elevator operator at the Upson Nut Works, and in November that year, the family took up residence in a rented house on Cleveland's West Side.

The house in question, 11 Horace Street, was rather small and sat against an unnamed alley at the west end of a large lot on the north side of Horace. The east end of the property was occupied by a much larger house that fronted Green Street, presently West 33rd Street. The big yard was exactly what the Burcharts were looking for. It was ideal for their children to play in and for the chickens they intended to raise. In the spring, they planned to put in a garden.

Joining them in their home was a boarder named William F. Kruger, who was employed as a fireman. Late nights often found Charles and Will playing cards in the living room. On one particular night, just over three weeks after taking up residency in the small home, Mrs. Burchart retired to bed, leaving her husband and the boarder to their card game. As she lay in bed, her thoughts drifted to her two children in the West. Suddenly, she had the uncomfortable feeling of being watched. With a start, she looked toward the widow and there saw the form of a man standing just on the other side of the glass. According to her description, the man had black hair and a face of extreme whiteness. He wore a stiff hat, a light shirt, an overcoat and black trousers.

When Mrs. Burchart composed herself enough to let out a scream, the figure glided across the yard and passed through the door of a small shed on their property. Continuing through the back wall of the shed, it reemerged in the yard and entered a neighbor's property, where it passed through the wall of another outbuilding. Sleeping that night was impossible, and the adults in the house stayed up into the late hours discussing the strange event.

The story of what had transpired was not shared with the children, yet the next morning, they seemed uneasy. When asked what was troubling them, they said that they didn't know but that something was queer about the house. This was where the troubles started.

Over the next few weeks, the family continued to experience unusual phenomena. Mysterious groans were heard at times when no one else was about. Doors started to open and close on their own. Lights and shadows were seen to flicker and move across the walls and ceiling. Word spread throughout the neighborhood of what was going on in the Burcharts' cottage. Two of the neighboring women kindly offered holy water and a rosary, which Mrs. Burchart accepted. Placing those items in her home seemed to work for about three weeks, but in time, the troubles returned.

As Mrs. Burchart and her daughter were engaged in cleaning the house one day, her daughter went to remove the ashpan from the fire and burned her finger on the hot stove. She cursed at the pain, and almost instantly, a sneering voice coming from beneath the stove laughed out the words, "Ya ya!" The voice was plainly heard by both Mrs. Burchart and her daughter. In haste, they tore from the room and ran to the house next door. From then on, neither would remain in the house alone.

One night, while sitting in their bedroom, Mr. and Mrs. Burchart observed a glowing light in the upper corner of the room. No lamp was burning, but the eerie light lingered for some time. Finally, it moved across the ceiling and vanished. On another night, the Burcharts' daughter was resting on the couch and suddenly started screaming. She claimed that there was some creature under the bed and that it had glared at her with catlike eyes.

On a Saturday toward the end of February 1903, Mrs. Burchart and her daughter were visiting the Grimms, who occupied the large house that fronted on Green Street at the other end of the property. From the back room, the Burchart house could plainly be seen. Casting a glance at the small house, Mrs. Burchart, her daughter and Mrs. Grimm all saw a light appear inside the Burchart home. It was thought that Will Kruger had returned home and was striking a match to light a pipe. Mrs. Grimm sent one of her sons over to investigate. When he returned, he said that no one was there. At this, Mrs. Burchart and her daughter went to take a second look but likewise found the house empty. When they returned to the Grimm house, they looked out the back window and again witnessed the same light reigniting.

In time, the Burcharts' daughter finally said what everyone in the neighborhood was already thinking: that the house was, in fact, haunted. It wasn't long before the Burchart home was being referred to as the Haunted House. Some in the neighborhood went as far as to declare that the devil himself was visiting that cottage. One morning, when the ground was soft, Mrs. Burchart discovered what appeared to be a cow's hoofprint beneath her window. She thought this impossible, as the gate was too narrow to admit an animal of that size. What's more, there was only the one track. She reached out to a neighbor to ask for her opinion on what the print might be. At this, the woman shrieked that Satan himself had visited their home, and she fled from the yard in terror. From then on, most of the neighbors avoided the house entirely.

To some, the idea of supernatural agents visiting the Burchart home was beyond them, and other explanations for the disturbances were offered. When the police were notified of what was transpiring, their thought was that someone was attempting to steal the Burcharts' chickens. A patrolman was sent to keep an eye on the house, and the chickens were secured at night. A few of the neighbors were of the mind that some treasure had been secreted away in the house and that attempts were being made by parties unknown to claim it. Some even went as far as to allege that an area "witch" had taken offense against the owner of the house and cursed the property to the point that it couldn't be rented.

Explanations and sending police to watch the house did little to change the matter. The disturbances continued and with the same frequency. The Burcharts were of the mind that if a reasonable explanation couldn't be found, they'd have to move. Their lease, which was for a term of one year, was the biggest issue. They were obliged to pay their rent, whether they lived in that house or not. As it was, the children had vowed not to remain in the house, preferring to leave their parents and live elsewhere than stay any longer.

HAUNTED HOUSE ON HORACE STREET.

The Burchart home on Horace Street was said to be the scene of a haunting. *From the Cleveland Leader, 1903.*

Eventually, the Burcharts had reached their breaking point. They abandoned the house on Horace Street and moved with Will Kruger into another home just around the corner on what's now Fulton Road.

All in all, the neighbors were somewhat baffled as to what could have been the cause of the haunting on Horace Street. None recalled any terrible tragedy happening in that place. One neighbor who was more vocal than most was Henry J. Hill, who'd owned and occupied the large house at the opposite end of the lot on Green Street from 1871 until the early 1880s. According to Hill, the house at 11 Horace Street was built about thirty years earlier by the Lutheran Band, a musical organization that used the building for meetings. Henry and his wife, Kate, even lived in it briefly before selling the property to the next owners, George and Anna Chapman. In 1896, the Chapmans sold the property to their daughter, Marguerite, who owned it at the time the haunting was reported.

The Lutheran Band likewise used the little house only into the early 1880s. After being purchased by the Chapmans, it saw use as a rental, just as was the case when the Burcharts and Will Kruger occupied it. As far as

A present-day view of Hancock Avenue, formerly Horace Street. *Photo by William G. Krejci.*

tragedies go, no reported violent acts or murders occurred there, yet the house did witness a couple of deaths. The first of these occurred just over twenty years prior to the events of 1903. On June 15, 1882, three-year-old Maria Herrman, a daughter of Mathias Herrman, died in the house from measles. The other death occurred on January 3, 1894, when Fred Queasbarth, a seven-month-old son of August and Mary Ann Queasbarth, died of inanition, or severe malnutrition.

Three years after the events that drove the Burcharts from their home, Horace Street was renamed Hancock Avenue, and the name Horace was applied to the small alley immediately to the south. The little cottage at 11 Horace Street and the large house that fronted Green Street were purchased by the noted developer Philip H. Marquard in December 1906 and demolished shortly after. By 1908, the old structures were replaced by a row of five beautiful homes. The site of the Horace Street haunting is currently occupied by a house that sits on the northeast corner of Hancock Avenue and West 34th Place.

CHAPTER 24

TO DIG WITHIN A CELLAR

41.50706, -81.68456

Like some dripping cavern, the chambers of the house were haunted by an
incessant echoing, which filled the air and mingled with the ticking of the clocks.
—The Strange Case of Dr. Jekyll and Mr. Hyde
by Robert Louis Stevenson

Around the beginning of November 1903, occupancy of the two-story building situated at 603 St. Clair Avenue was taken up by Charles L. Vedder; his wife, Mary; and her two children from her first marriage. Vedder operated a used furniture store on the first floor of the building and reserved the second as the family residence. The Vedders weren't in the home long before they were aroused in the night by strange noises about the premises.

At first, they thought nothing of the matter and hoped it would settle in time, but the noises continued, and the family soon found it difficult to sleep. Things were being thrown about the place, and doors were slamming on their own. The Vedders' seventeen-year-old daughter, Lizzie, said that she was awakened at two o'clock in the morning by a cold hand over her face. When she opened her eyes, she saw a large man covered in blood standing at the foot of her bed, smiling at her. When she screamed, the visitor vanished. A few nights later, she was awakened by a cold hand touching her forehead. Again, she opened her eyes to see the large man standing in her room. He was quiet but had a sorrowful look on his face. When she screamed, her parents came running into the room, but as was the case before, the man vanished.

1547 St. Clair Avenue, formerly 603 St. Clair Street, circa 1945. *Photo courtesy Cleveland Public Library Photograph Collection.*

Mary Vedder explained that when the family awoke in the morning, they'd find items on their table moved around. Sometimes their dishes were found on the floor and the furniture out of place. On one occasion, the stove door was heard slamming shut. Thinking burglars had entered their home, the Vedders searched the place with a revolver but could find no one there. What's more, there were no tracks outside in the snow leading to or from their home.

When word got out about what was transpiring at the Vedders' home, some suggested that the place might be haunted by the ghost of Mr. Shipherd, who went missing almost eight months earlier.

David Chester Shipherd and his wife, Carrie, previously operated a dairy at 603 St. Clair, where Vedder's secondhand furniture store was located. On May 18, 1903, Carrie Shipherd was going to visit the grave of her son and informed her husband that she shouldn't be long. He told her not to hurry, as she'd be quite alone when she got back. On her return to the store, her husband was nowhere to be found. He'd made up the books, left his keys in the money drawer and vanished completely. For reasons unknown, Carrie Shipherd waited nearly a month to report her husband missing. In the meantime, she and her brother-in-law continued the dairy business until they were forced to close. Carrie Shipherd then moved to Central Avenue and put the place on St. Clair up for rent.

It was now being suggested by some of the neighbors that David Shipherd had actually been murdered and that his rotting corpse lay buried in the basement. The police received the tip regarding the possibility of David Shipherd's whereabouts and quietly sent over a team to look into the matter. The dig was headed up by detectives Frank G. Wood and Andrew A. Ryan, assisted by Sergeant John F. Reiber and Patrolman William A. Bitzer of the Second Precinct.

After two days of digging, all that was excavated was an empty box and some bricks. Charles Vedder, still believing that the paranormal activity originated from somewhere in the cellar, ended up placing a large and heavy stove over the trapdoor in hopes of preventing ghosts from entering their place. In the end, the Vedders broke their two-year lease with Carrie Shipherd and moved to another building up the road on St. Clair.

As it turned out, David C. Shipherd wasn't murdered, nor was his body secreted away beneath the cellar of 603 St. Clair Avenue. The truth of the matter was that he'd simply left his wife and was hiding out at his parents' farm in Bainbridge. He and Carrie divorced soon after. He remarried in 1910 and died seven years later. Honestly, nothing even resembling a murder had ever occurred at the house on St. Clair. The only person known to have died at that address was four-month-old Peppie Greenberger, daughter of a past occupant named Simon Greenberger, who died of pneumonia in early August 1882.

When Cleveland streets were renamed and houses renumbered in 1906, the address of 603 St. Clair was changed to 1547. Having been built in the mid-1860s, that building stood for nearly one hundred years and was ultimately demolished during the second half of the twentieth century. A modern building now stands on the site.

CHAPTER 25
THE HAUNTED INN
AT THE SHAKER SETTLEMENT

41.44541, -81.49739

*There was manifestly nothing in the external appearance of this particular house
to bear out the tales of the horror that was said to reign within.*
—The Empty House *by Algernon Blackwood*

I t's commonly accepted that old inns are a favorite location for ghosts to dwell. Much like those spooky old houses at the end of the street that have been empty for years, these former stagecoach stops are the perfect setting for tales of murder and woe.

One of the earliest such stories comes from the Toledo area, where in 1885, an old tavern and hotel was drawing attention for its otherworldly activity. Its location was never actually given. The article simply placed it not far from that city, on a road passing through a well-improved part of the country. The building in question had two wings and was known locally as the Haunted House.

The story related here occurred about fifty years earlier, when the establishment was under the proprietorship of a man simply referred to as Goster. Of course, no one with that name can be located in any records as having resided in that area. Still, the story goes on to say that Goster's hotel was visited one evening by a well-dressed stranger who was carrying a large amount of cash. The man took a room for the night but was never seen again.

The following morning, the man's horse was found wandering the road, but no trace of its rider was ever found. A year or two later, an advertisement appeared in the newspaper stating that a man, whose name was withheld, had set out from Connecticut with a large sum of money to purchase land. He sent regular reports of his progress, but after the man departed Cleveland, the letters stopped coming. It was widely suspected that Goster had something to do with the man's disappearance, though nothing was done to pursue the matter. It was also said that, some years later, as Goster lay on his deathbed in great agony, he tried to confess to something but was unable to speak and died before he could clear his conscience. Another claim was made that a man had caught Goster in the act of burying the body in the cellar, but Goster paid him $1,000 to remain silent.

As for the old inn, it sat empty and deserted for many years. In that time, the ghostly tales emerged. It was said that eerie sights and sounds were frequently experienced. Some said that the sound of a hammer striking a coffin lid had been heard about the place for the last fifty years. It was also claimed that music of incomparable sweetness was heard to drift from room to room in the dead of night. The door to the room where the traveler met his grisly fate refused to stay closed. Not two minutes after being shut, it would fly open again, no matter what was placed in front of it. Of course, the hotel has its phantoms and specters as well. In fact, this wayside inn had all the trappings of a typical late-nineteenth-century haunted house.

That story may sound familiar. Some variation on it has been told about most haunted inns, taverns and hotels. But why talk of a haunted hotel in northwest Ohio when this book is focused on the greater Cleveland area? In truth, that story was related in order to better explain this next one.

In the spring of 1908, a medium, referred to only as Mrs. Paine, was interviewed by Karl Kingsley Kitchen, a reporter for the *Plain Dealer*, regarding her experiences with ghosts. The woman claimed to have investigated them for years and, in consequence, had many encounters with those who have traveled beyond the grave. Near the end of her lengthy account on the subject, Mrs. Paine recalled how a few years earlier, she visited a house near the Shaker Settlement that was said to have been the scene of a murder many years before. In that case, a man had murdered his own son. Strange noises had been heard throughout the house, and strange forms were seen at the window of the room where the crime was said to have been committed.

Mrs. Paine arrived at the house and settled in for the evening. It wasn't long before she was convinced that the building was, in fact, haunted by the ghost of the murdered man. She saw nothing until around midnight. It was then that she felt herself seized by an unseen hand and heard a

A view of the Shaker Settlement, circa 1905. *Photo courtesy Cleveland Public Library Photograph Collection.*

voice that seemed to say, "You had better leave me." The room was flushed with a whitish-green haze, but in a few minutes, the light faded and the manifestation disappeared.

So now, we may wonder: where was this haunted house located, and who was this barbarous villain that would murder his own son? An article from 1906, also written by Karl Kitchen, gives the answer.

Near the settlement of the North Union Shakers in present-day Shaker Heights, there once stood a very large inn, built of hand-hewn beams and clapboard siding. Popular with farmers on their way to and from the markets at Cleveland, the affair was owned and operated by one Josiah White, who lived in the building with his wife and two sons. The inn saw much success at first, but in time, White took to gambling and lost most of his profits. It's said that he was caught cheating with loaded dice and marked cards. Afterward, few travelers chose to stay there, and Josiah White was soon in financial ruin. He'd mortgaged his inn and was facing eviction.

On the night of September 6, 1843, Josiah White's inn was visited by John Wilmont, a wealthy farmer from near Gates Mills. Wilmont had passed through the day before with a herd of cattle for the market in Cleveland.

Having sold his herd, he was returning with several hundred dollars on his person. It being too late to continue the journey home, Wilmont took a room at White's. Before going to his room, he ordered a nightcap in the taproom. When he went to pay for his drink, White observed the vast amount of money that Wilmont had in the purse on his leather belt.

After finishing his drink, White showed Wilmont to a room on the second floor in the front of the house. Wilmont securely locked the bedroom door, tucked his money belt under his pillow and, in ten minutes, was fast asleep. He was awakened not two hours later by the sound of someone outside his bedroom window. Fearing that it might be a thief, he grabbed the money belt and crawled into a wardrobe on the other side of the room. Carefully hidden in the clothes press, he kept the door slightly ajar so that he could see what was transpiring. A few minutes later, a young man appeared on the ledge outside. After struggling for some time, he managed to pry open the window and entered. He immediately disrobed and crawled into the bed.

Before he could decide whether to alert White of the intruder or eject the man from the bed himself, Wilmont heard footsteps coming up the stairs toward his room. The person reached the door but found it locked. Suddenly, as if by magic, the bedroom door swung open, and a large man stood silhouetted in the entrance. The door, apparently, had a hidden hinge and latch that could be opened from the outside when it was locked from within.

Wilmont watched quietly as the man entered the room and stood near the bed. With the moonlight streamed into the room, Wilmont could now see that it was Josiah White—and what's more, that he held a large butcher's knife in his hand. Standing over the sleeping figure in the bed, White plunged the knife into his unsuspecting victim's breast, piercing the heart and killing him instantly.

On witnessing the horrible crime, John Wilmont fainted, and it was many minutes before he regained consciousness. When he came to, he thought that he'd dreamed the entire event. Looking over at the bed, he found it empty, but on closer inspection discovered the telltale pool of blood that soaked the mattress. At this, he hastily dressed, put the money belt around his waist and escaped out the window that the young man had entered through.

Running as fast as his legs would allow, John Wilmont awakened the neighbors with shouts of murder. In time, a large party had gathered, armed themselves and proceeded to White's inn. When they arrived, they found the front door locked but plainly heard Josiah White on the other side sobbing and calling out his son John's name. They attempted to break down the door, but a few moments later, the door opened and there before them stood Josiah White in a state of absolute grief. In his hands he held a pistol. A couple of the neighbors reached out to take it from him, but before they could grab it, White raised it to his temple and pulled the trigger, ending his own life instantly. Behind him lay the lifeless body of his son, John.

From what could be gathered, John White had ridden to Cleveland earlier in the evening and returned drunk. Trying to avoid detection by his father, the young man climbed up the front of the building and, not knowing that the front room was occupied, entered the window and crawled into the bed. Josiah White went upstairs and entered the room with the intention of killing John Wilmont and taking his money but instead murdered his own son. He carried the body downstairs, planning to bury it behind the house, but when he reached the bottom of the stairs, he learned the truth of his actions and there sat grieving until the neighbors arrived.

The article closed by saying that Josiah White and his son were buried by the Shakers in their little graveyard. Mrs. White and her surviving son moved away, and the old inn was afterward used by the Shakers as a general store. It was one of the last buildings to be torn down when the site of the North Union Settlement was sold to developers.

That story may also sound familiar. It very much mirrors the tale that was shared in Toledo in 1885, minus the part about the owner's son being the victim of the murder. The tale of the murder was also included fairly recently in a book on true crime in Cleveland.

Unfortunately, the story of Josiah White and John Wilmont is just that: a story. No evidence exists to support that it ever occurred. Neither Josiah White nor John Wilmont appear in any records for Cuyahoga County. Also, one would think that such a terrible crime would be covered by the Cleveland newspapers when it occurred. It wasn't. Nor was it covered in any other newspaper. In fact, there isn't even an obituary anywhere for Josiah White or his son. The coroner case files from this era don't report anyone named White dying by either murder or suicide, nor do they list anyone else by any other name dying by those causes in September 1843.

So, what then, is the origin of this story?

In many ways, it's a mix of two stories. The leading elements are drawn from the tale of the haunted old inn that was reported on in Toledo in 1885. The rest is pulled from a real crime that occurred in Warrensville Township in 1868. The details of that are as follows.

On the eastern edge of Warrensville Township sat the sixty-seven-acre farm of James and Elizabeth Quayle. The two had been married in 1845

Various headlines that relate to the legend, murder and haunting at the Shaker Settlement. *From the* Cleveland Leader, *1868, and the* Plain Dealer, *1906 and 1908.*

and to them were born three sons named Edward, Henry and Silas, and a daughter named Jane. James Quayle was tragically hit and killed by a streetcar on January 1, 1861, and was laid to rest at Warrensville East Cemetery, now called Beachwood Cemetery. Two years later, Elizabeth was married to a merchant sailor originally from the Isle of Man named John "Jack" Coole. On the death of James Quayle, the farm passed to his wife and children in equal shares. Coole managed to acquire the shares belonging to his wife and stepdaughter but was looking to control the entire affair. He didn't bother much with Silas, who was only nine years old, but was actively trying to persuade Edward and Henry, who were eighteen and twenty, respectively, to sign over their shares to him. They refused this, which greatly drew his ire. In May 1868, Jack Coole was charged with assault and battery of his older stepsons and was fined fifteen dollars. At this, the boys moved to the farm of a neighbor named Joseph Thorpe. The following month, they signed documents naming Thorpe as their guardian; thus, their shares of the farm couldn't be touched by Jack Coole. That was the final straw.

On Saturday, June 27, 1868, the Quayle brothers traveled to Cleveland with Thorpe and Coole to settle the matter with attorneys for good, but while there, Jack Coole got drunk and refused all terms. With no progress made, all parties returned to Warrensville. Coole spent that evening in the barn sharpening his butcher's knife. At around eight o'clock that night, he encountered Edward and Henry on the road near their home and attacked them with the knife. He first went after Henry, who was almost completely disemboweled. Henry managed to run about fifty feet before collapsing beside the road. Edward intervened but was likewise stabbed multiple times. Henry died from his wounds about four hours later. The following morning, Edward Quayle made a statement that read:

> *I Edward Quayle of Warrensville, Cuyahoga County, Ohio upon oath do make this my dying statement, on this Sunday morning June 28, 1868.*
>
> *I am about twenty years old. My physicians tell me I cannot live but a short time. I believe this to be true, and that I must soon die of the wounds that I received last night about 8 o'clock.*
>
> *I was stabbed last night in this town and county about 8 o'clock by John Cool who married my mother. He stabbed me and my brother Henry with a butcher knife. My brother is dead.*
>
> *The final thing that John Cool said to me when he met me was that he was going to kill me. He did not say what for. As soon as he said this he stabbed us. I tried to get away from him—he stabbed me. My brother interfered to help me and John Cool stabbed him.*
>
> *He stabbed me six times.*
>
> *John Cool has often previous to last night threatened to kill me. Edward Quayle X his mark*

Edward Quayle died from his wounds on Monday morning. Both of the boys were laid to rest beside their father at Beachwood Cemetery. Their graves are unmarked.

After committing the horrific deed, Jack Coole returned to his house and barricaded himself inside with a loaded gun. The neighbors surrounded the place to prevent his escape while police were sent for in Cleveland. When the police arrived, they forced their way into the home. In true Josiah White fashion, Coole turned his gun on himself in an attempt to end his life; however, the shot had fallen out of the barrel and all that he managed to do was scorch the side of his face with the blast of burning gunpowder.

Jack Coole was arrested and charged with the murders of his stepsons, though he never saw trial. On July 7, the first day of the trial, Coole managed to acquire a razor from another inmate. That night, he successfully took his life by cutting his own throat. It was said that Coole was buried at Woodland Cemetery beside Dr. John W. Hughes, who was hanged in February 1866 for the murder of Tamzen Parsons. This appears to be in error, as newspaper articles claimed that Hughes was buried instead in an unmarked grave at Erie Street Cemetery. Coole's grave in section 31, lot 27 at Woodland is likewise unmarked.

By 1916, the Quayle property had been purchased by the City of Cleveland, and it was incorporated into the Cooley Farm Plan for the use

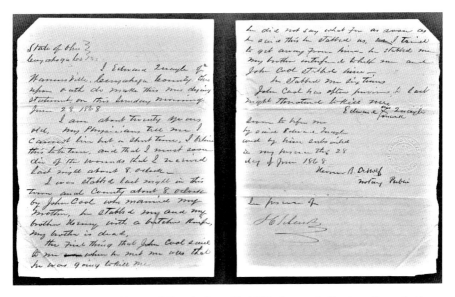

The dying statement of Edward Quayle, June 28, 1868. *Courtesy the Cuyahoga County Archives.*

of the new corrections facility. The Quayle house ended up being used as a hog house and was torn down in the 1930s. The site of the house, as well as the horrific murder of the Quayle brothers, is now the parking lot for the Harvard Park Shopping Center on Richmond Road.

As far as the Haunted Inn at the Shaker Settlement goes, it may have existed. There certainly must have been a building that inspired Karl Kitchen to spin his tale, and yes, it may have originally been used as an inn. It may even have been haunted, just as Mrs. Paine claimed. One thing we can be certain of, though: it wasn't haunted by a young man who was murdered in bed by his father, as neither person ever existed.

CHAPTER 26
THE GILLSY GUEST

41.50148, -81.68764

I know that ghosts have *wandered on earth. Be with me always—take any form—drive me mad! only* do *not leave me in this abyss, where I cannot find you! Oh God! It is unutterable! I* cannot *live without my life! I* cannot *live without my soul!*
—Wuthering Heights *by Emily Brontë*

Sidney C. Mayer was born in March 1877 in Oil City, Venango County, Pennsylvania, to German immigrants Ludwig and Frederika Mayer. He attended school in Oil City and afterward did a stint in the U.S. Army during the Spanish American War. He served as a private in Company A of the 41st U.S. Volunteer Infantry from October 1899 until January 1901, at which time he was honorably discharged. He returned to Oil City, where he took work as a traveling salesman.

His ramblings brought him to the town of Tonawanda, New York, where he made the acquaintance of twenty-year-old Vera Ilna Compton. A romance ensued, and on August 9, 1908, the two were married in Buffalo. After the wedding, the newlyweds took up residency in Detroit, where Sidney had recently been hired as a representative of a hardware concern.

On October 7, they moved into a rooming house at 39 Columbia Street. Sidney went out on the road again for the next four days and returned that Sunday to be with his wife. That evening, the two got into a fight, which ended with Vera telling Sidney that she was leaving him and returning to her parents in New York. He pleaded with her not to leave, but the following morning, she departed, leaving a forwarding address with the proprietor of the rooming house.

Five days later, Sidney Mayer arrived in Cleveland and took a room at the Gillsy Hotel, a relatively new accommodation located at 1811 East 9th Street. Not long after checking in, Mayer started writing letters to his wife, to which there were no replies. He sent a telegram the following Thursday that went unanswered. The hotel staff noticed that he seemed to be acting queerly, as though he were on the verge of nervous prostration. It was then that Sidney Mayer declared to the staff and management that the Gillsy Hotel was haunted.

Mayer claimed to have witnessed apparitions and shapes that peered at him from down the corridors and through the windows of his room. In some cases, it was just a strange noise in the hallway. Other times it was a specter that chased him relentlessly about the place.

When this was brought to the attention of Robert E. Gill, proprietor of the Gillsy, he had Mayer relocated to a room where no noise could be heard and no one could access the windows. Still, Mayer continued to witness the strange manifestations, and each time he did, his room was changed. This occurred no less than four times in two days.

On the evening of Wednesday, October 21, Sidney Mayer was seen about the hotel, but the following morning, he didn't come out of his room. The staff went to check on him but found the room locked and thought it best to let him sleep. That Friday morning, the room was still locked, and no one had seen or heard from Mayer. Not being able to enter through the locked door, a bellboy was lowered from the window of the room above. He crawled into Mayer's room though the window and there found the man deceased.

Mayer's body was undressed and lying half on the bed. A .38-caliber revolver with two empty chambers lay beside the body. By the best guesses that could be made based on the position of the body, he'd been standing in front of the mirror when he shot himself in the head. Several letters were found in his pocket, one being from his wife. Sidney C. Mayer was thirty-one. The remains were conveyed to Hogan & Company's morgue and then sent back to Pennsylvania, where he was buried at Mount Zion Cemetery in Franklin, Venango County.

Vera Mayer remained a widow until she remarried eight years later and moved to Georgia, where she died in 1985 at the age of ninety-seven.

It's an interesting thought that a man would believe a one-year-old hotel to be haunted. In that first year, no deaths had occurred in the place, nor

The Gillsy Hotel, circa 1915. *Photo courtesy Cleveland Public Library Photograph Collection.*

were there any tragic accidents during the construction phase. In fact, the only incident of note in the hotel up until that point was a small fire that broke out in the telephone exchange room in December 1907. Curiously, advertisements boasted that the hotel was fireproof.

In cases like this, a search of the history of the site can reveal more of the story.

George W. Howe. *From* History of Cuyahoga County, Ohio, *1879.*

The first building known to grace the site was built and occupied by William Given in 1862. It was a three-story brick structure with a basement. The front of the house was finished ornately in sandstone. During those earliest years, the house carried the address 150 Erie Street, but later, the address was changed to 225 Erie.

William Given remained in the home for only two years. In 1864, he sold it to George William Howe, a prominent Cleveland railroad investor and mercantile operator, who served as Cleveland police commissioner and later as collector for the U.S. Customs House in Cleveland. The Erie Street home served as a residence for Howe and his wife, Katherine, as well as his many in-laws. George Howe also built a fine residence on Euclid Avenue's Millionaire's Row, which today exists as Parker-Hannifin Hall. George Howe died there in 1901.

And while no horrific deaths occurred at the Erie Street house, it certainly saw its share of passings. Four people are known to have concluded their lives at that address. All were in-laws of George W. Howe. William H. Sholl, Howe's brother-in-law, died on August 8, 1878, at the age of fifty-five. On September 10, 1884, Catherine Lemen, George Howe's seventy-four-year-old mother-in-law, also passed in the house. March 8, 1892, saw the passing of Anna Lemen-Sholl, wife and daughter of the previously mentioned William and Catherine. Five months later, Anna's sister Mary Morrison died in the home from blood poisoning.

George W. Howe sold the house in 1893 and moved to his residence on Euclid. That year, tenancy was picked up by William L. Otis, who used it as a furniture and pottery store. It was also that year that the building first saw use as a clubhouse for the Rowfant Club. Another part of the house was rented as a residence to Ora W. Williams, who remained until 1897. By 1901, the house was vacant, and by 1904, it had been demolished. Three years later, the Gillsy Hotel opened on the site.

While no tragedies occurred in the short year that the Gillsy was open that might have accounted for the apparitions witnessed by Sidney Mayer, one tragedy involving an employee did follow only days after his suicide. Robert Donnelly, a thirty-one-year-old bartender who worked at the Gillsy,

The Howe Residence, 255 Erie Street, circa 1904. *Photo courtesy Cleveland Public Library Photograph Collection.*

fell ill and was brought to the emergency room at the hospital in a state of delirium. As he was being carried inside, he broke free and ran back out of the hospital but tripped down the steps and broke his neck. He was carried back inside but died a few minutes later.

The Gillsy Hotel continued a run of success for almost fifty years but was demolished in 1954. Today, the site is occupied by Ohio Savings Plaza at 1801 East 9th Street.

CHAPTER 27

SHE WARNS OF DOOM

41.51169, -81.66699

*The servant-maid gasped for breath, and wrung her hands with fear. I sprung to
my feet, when Janet's face—it was the face of a ghost!—warned me back.*
—A Woman's Ransom *by Frederick William Robinson*

At 1:13 on the morning of November 28, 1900, northbound train
No. 301 on the Cleveland & Pittsburgh Railroad left the tracks near
Beaver, Pennsylvania, and plunged into the icy Ohio River with
nearly one hundred passengers aboard. A recent flood had undermined the
approach to the river crossing near the confluence of the Ohio and Beaver
Rivers, and the weight of the locomotive caused the tracks to give way. The
train consisted of a sleeper car, two coaches, an express car and a mail and
baggage car. All of these were pulled by Engine No. 611.

As the locomotive dropped into the river, the fireman jumped clear and
never received so much as a scratch. The engineer, on the other hand, stuck
to his post and rode the engine all the way down into the river. In doing
so, his right leg was pinned and crushed. Ultimately freeing himself, the
engineer climbed from the wreckage, entered the frigid Ohio and swam for
the nearest shore. As he pulled himself up the bank, he noticed the state
of his leg and tended to it at once, pulling off his shirt and tying it into a
tourniquet just below his knee. He lost consciousness a few minutes later but
was discovered by one of the passengers, a man named Chapin. When the
engineer awoke, the only thing he asked Chapin was if the passengers were
safe. They were. In fact, not one of the passengers had been killed or injured
in the wreck.

Much can be said of the bravery of those early railroading men. Working the rail lines was a risky occupation, more so than today. When an engineer can keep a cool head and stick to his post in the face of disaster, he should certainly be acknowledged. And so he shall be. In this case, his name was Albert L. Coughenour of Cleveland. Coughenour, age fifty-two, had worked since the age of twenty for the Cleveland & Pittsburgh Railroad. He kept a home at 1803, later renumbered 3346, Superior Street with his wife, Julia, and children Margaret and Ernest.

In all, there were only five casualties accounted for that November night in 1900, truly a miracle under the circumstances. The others injured, beside Coughenour, were baggage master James Allen, conductor Frank Connelly and Pullman car porter John Taylor. Sadly, one man was killed, that being Michael S. Casey, the express messenger, who was the only person riding in the express car. That car was washed away in the swollen waters of the Ohio and was located some forty-eight miles downstream the following day.

The injured Coughenour was taken back to Cleveland and, on his return, was admitted to the hospital. The doctors determined that his injuries were too severe, and the engineer's right leg was amputated below the knee. When receiving the news of the accident, Coughenour's wife wasn't the least bit surprised. She claimed that at the same time the accident was occurring, she awoke in her Cleveland bed to the sound of her husband's voice calling out to her. At this, she rose from the bed and unbolted the bedroom door, thinking that he was in the hallway and couldn't get in, but the corridor was empty. Knowing that something terrible had happened to her husband, she remained awake the rest of the night and, shortly after sunrise, received word of the accident.

After recovering from his injuries, Coughenour returned to work for the Cleveland & Pittsburgh Railroad. As previously stated, it was dangerous work, but the seasoned railroader had experience on his side.

Tragedy struck the Coughenour family on October 20, 1906. On that day, Albert and Julia Coughenour's daughter Margaret died at their home quite suddenly. Earlier that year, she'd been married to a man named John Addleman and had recently given birth to their daughter, Rhea. The funeral was held at their home, and her burial took place at Lake View Cemetery.

In August 1912, Margaret returned to them. It happened one evening six years after her passing, while Albert and Julia Coughenour were sitting together in their home: the voice of their deceased daughter sounded clearly in their ears.

"I see a railroad wreck," said the voice. "I see Papa in it. I will protect him." And just like that, the voice departed.

On a Wednesday night, two weeks later, as the Coughenours were asleep in their bed, the voice returned. This time, it spoke only to Julia Coughenour and again warned of a coming disaster. It was with much hesitation that Albert Coughenour set out early that Friday morning, August 30, aboard the No. 307 on his regular run to Pittsburgh.

The train arrived safely in Pittsburgh, but as it did, a minor derailment occurred near the rail yard at Conway, Pennsylvania, about twenty miles behind them. In that case, several freight cars derailed while entering the rail yard. A wrecking car was brought in, and work to clear the line commenced.

Meanwhile, Julia Coughenour was sitting back at her Superior Street home in Cleveland when she suddenly witnessed the apparition of her daughter dressed in a misty white robe. In each hand, she held out a rose. When she spoke, she simply said, "It is all over," and vanished. One hour later, the tragic news was received.

As the No. 307 made its return trip to Cleveland, it entered a bank of fog near Conway and failed to see that the wrecking car's crane was extended

The Conway train wreck in August 1912. *Beaver County Genealogy and History Center.*

over the passenger rail line. The locomotive collided with the crane, causing the passenger train to derail. In all, four men were killed and seven others badly injured. Among the dead was Albert L. Coughenour. Curiously, this wreck occurred only four miles from the scene of the disaster in 1900.

Albert Coughenour was laid to rest near his daughter at Lake View Cemetery. From what is known, his departed daughter never again visited the Coughenour home. The family ultimately moved out in 1921, and the home was demolished a few years later. It was replaced by a brick commercial building that still stands on the site where the ghost of Margaret Coughenour-Addleman once warned of doom.

CHAPTER 28

THE OLD CLEVELAND WORKHOUSE

41.48678, –81.63411

Around him swarm the plaining ghosts
Like those on Virgil's shore—
A wilderness of faces dim,
And pale ones gashed and hoar.
—*"In the Prison Pen" by Herman Melville*

Just southwest of the intersection of Woodland Avenue and East 79th Street sat a large and imposing structure that loomed high above the surrounding neighborhood. Greatly resembling an impenetrable fortress, the massive stone building featured towers, turrets and crenelated battlements. The beautifully manicured grounds were a stark contrast to the dark and formidable edifice and did little to erase the sense of fear it cast into the hearts of those who were ordered to dwell withing its dark gray walls. This was the Cleveland Workhouse.

Believe it or not, there was a time when a person could be locked up just for being destitute. These places were also referred to as poorhouses and almshouses. The first city workhouse existed as part of the Cleveland City Infirmary on the West Side and was established in the mid-1850s. On March 1, 1871, the new facility on Woodland opened as the Cleveland Workhouse and House of Refuge and Corrections. It housed not only Cleveland's indigent population but also petty offenders and the wayward of the city. The two front wings, each of which were four hundred feet long, contained four tiers of jail cells. The compound also contained a female refuge and

The Cleveland Workhouse, circa 1875. *Photo courtesy Cleveland Public Library Photograph Collection.*

prison and a boys' refuge. As its primary function was that of a workhouse, the southwest wing contained a large brush-making factory.

When the workhouse was first opened, the city hailed it as "the finest looking, best arranged, most extensive and least expensive building of its kind in the United States." One of the reasons it was built at such a grand scale was that Cleveland was trying to show up Cincinnati, which four years earlier, had also built a large workhouse. Cleveland's was twice the size.

After forty-one years of operation, the Cleveland Workhouse was closed, and the last prisoners were transferred to the new Workhouse Farm at the Warrensville House of Corrections on September 9, 1912. In its time, the building had housed a total of 96,496 inmates.

As the last inmates were getting ready to depart, some stopped to share a few stories of the old workhouse with one or two members of the press who were there to cover the story. Among the tales shared that morning were stories of two parts of the building where, it was said, spirits from beyond the grave dwelt. One story told of a guard who committed suicide in his room some fifteen years earlier. Another yarn spoke of "a swarthy, baleful-eyed gypsy woman" who died in the women's dormitory. Since the deaths, both of those locations were said to be haunted. Of course, numerous deaths had occurred at that facility, primarily among the inmates. Some were from illness, and yes, some were from suicide. It's unknown who, exactly, the guard and the female inmate were.

Not surprisingly, the designer of this colossal Gothic Revival building was the renowned architect Levi Tucker Schofield. Interestingly, three other structures he designed are also reported to be haunted, these being the Soldiers and Sailors Monument on Cleveland's Public Square, the Ohio State Reformatory in Mansfield and the Athens Lunatic Asylum, also known as the Ridges.

Following its closure, the old workhouse was used by the Department of Public Utilities, specifically the waterworks department, which largely used the site for storage and a meter repair shop.

The land was eventually sold for redevelopment, and in October 1954, the demolition of the old workhouse commenced. Soon, all traces of the building were but a memory. On June 30, 1956, the newly completed Community Apartments complex opened on the site and received its first tenants.

CHAPTER 29
THE CAVE OF APPARITIONS

41.49071, -81.71221

Upon that night, when fairies light
On Cassilis Downans dance,
Or owre the lays, in splendid blaze,
On sprightly coursers prance;
Or for Colean the route is ta'en,
Beneath the moon's pale beams;
There, up the cove, to stray and rove,
Among the rocks and streams
To sport that night.
—"Halloween" by Robert Burns

As previously stated in this book, Bulkley Boulevard was constructed in 1912 along the lakeshore on Cleveland's West Side. Originally running from West 28th Street west to Edgewater Park, the road later crossed the river on the high-level Main Avenue Bridge and connected with Lakefront Road just north of Downtown. Today, we know this thoroughfare as the Shoreway.

Sadly, the construction of Bulkley came at the cost of losing a number of places that carried a haunted reputation. Among those were Patrick Smith's famed haunted house on the northwest corner of Pearl and Washington, Heffron's undertaking parlor where the ghost of Emily Frayne was said to scream from beyond the grave and Elias Sims's barn that later served as the haunted Patrol Station No. 2.

And yet, there's one more place to add to this list, that being the Cave of Apparitions.

Also referred to by some as the Haunted Archway, the Cave of Apparitions was a deep, stone-lined grotto cut into the hillside on the bluff high above the old riverbed. It was situated on the south side of Washington Avenue immediately west of a house that, in its final years, carried the address 2907 Washington. It's uncertain whether this was a naturally occurring void in the earth or if it was hewn out by the earliest owners of the property. One thing that all could agree on: it most certainly was haunted.

In December 1912, a reporter for the *Cleveland Leader* took a jaunt along the demolition site on Washington Avenue, where houses were being cleared for the construction of Bulkley. While there, he met up with two area residents who were likewise watching the neighborhood fall to progress.

Those who lived in the area were particularly happy to see the Cave of Apparitions go. According to Matt Corcoran of 2935 Washington Avenue, children didn't dare to pass it at night and adults who passed at those hours always asked for a blessing when doing so. Martin Mullen of 2818 Division Street claimed that the house at 2907 Washington was where Cleveland mayor Herman Baehr was born. The Baehr Distillery, he stated, sat just to the west of the house, and the cave beneath it had been haunted for years.

"Yes sir," Mullen declared, "I've heard people tell of seeing them. I've heard them lots of times, but I do not like to confess that I ever saw them. They are there, all right. And in a nice spring evening, the prettiest little fairies flit about the cavern."

"It has only been lately that I would go in the cave," added Matt Corcoran. "Lots of times I wouldn't even go by the place at night. All the people around here have seen the ghosts and fairies. So did I when I was little."

One could only wonder what it was about a hole in the earth that could strike fear on this scale into the hearts of those who dwelt near this geological anomaly.

The story of the Cave of Apparitions really begins in 1844, when a German immigrant named Matthias Mack purchased lot 168 of the former Charles Taylor Farm. At the time, Mack was residing in Medina County but had family already living in the Cleveland area. A few years after making his purchase, he built a fine brick home on the south side of the lot facing Vermont Street. Originally carrying the address 131 Vermont, it was ultimately changed to 2912 before being destroyed in 1912.

In the spring of 1849, Matthias Mack entered into a partnership with a man named C.C. Rogers and commenced in the lager-brewing trade under the name Rogers & Mack, but after only two months of operation, the firm was dissolved. In 1851, Mack reestablished a lager-brewing business on his own property. It was there that he built the Mack Brewery on the northeast corner of his lot at 341 Washington. With the establishment of this new brewery, he also opened a cooperage, or barrel-making shop, immediately to the east of his home on Vermont. The cooperage was short-lived, however, as it was completely destroyed by fire on October 10, 1854.

Mathias Mack either created the Cave of Apparitions himself or simply utilized an already existing gash in the earth. What is known for certain is that he used the hollowed space for storing his product at a cool temperature. In short, the Cave of Apparitions was a beer cellar.

Mack continued his brewery until his retirement in 1875 but passed away four years later. During the mid-1880s, the brewery building was torn down, but the cave on the site remained. In 1889, the brewery lot, cave included, was sold to Patrick and Anna English. Patrick, who operated a saloon on Whiskey Island, built a house immediately to the east of the cave entrance in 1890. Seven years later, the property was purchased by Magdalena Baehr, Cleveland's Madame Brewer.

Despite the claim made by Martin Mullen to the reporter from the *Cleveland Leader*, Cleveland mayor Herman Baehr was not born at that house. He was born in 1866 in Keokuk, Lee County, Iowa, where his parents, Jacob and Magdalena, were briefly residing. On their return to Cleveland the following year, the Baehrs opened a large brewing concern at 225 Pearl Street. The brewing facility operated on the first floor while the family occupied the second as their home. On Jacob Baehr's untimely death in 1873, his widow took over operations of the Baehr Brewery and continued to operate it successfully on her own for a quarter of a century.

When Magdalena Baehr purchased the old brewery site on Washington, she only used it for storing casks of beer in the haunted cave. Also contrary to Mullen's claim, the Baehrs didn't operate a distillery on the site. As Magdalena Baehr resided comfortably above her brewery on Pearl, she rented the house that sat to the east of the cave to the English family, who'd built it in 1890. Magdalena Baehr sold her brewery in 1898 and, two years later, relocated to Detroit Avenue, where she died in 1909. Her former brewery building on Pearl Street still stands and now carries the address 1526 West 25th Street. What's more, it again is being used for brewing purposes and is now the home of Bookhouse Brewing.

In 1911, Herman Baehr, who was administrator of his mother's estate, sold the house on Washington to a woman named Katherine Killius. For the

Left: Magdalena Baehr. *Photo courtesy Bookhouse Brewing.*

Below: On this site once sat the entrance to the Cave of Apparitions. *Photo by William G. Krejci.*

last few years, he had rented it to Edward and Mamie Burke, who, as it turned out, were the house's last occupants. The City of Cleveland purchased the lot, and those around it, in 1912 to make way for the new Bulkley Boulevard.

As far as any tragedies to have occurred on the site, only two are known. The first of these was the horrific death of Samuel Newcomb, a thirty-five-year-old German man, who was burned to death at Mack's Brewery on July 1, 1864. A veteran of the recent Civil War, he was survived by his wife, Elizabeth Hayden Newcomb. His remains were laid to rest at nearby Monroe Street Cemetery. The second incident occurred fewer than ten years later. On May 28, 1873, a sixteen-year-old boy named James Gallagher fell into the haunted cellar of the brewery and was so injured that it was worried his wounds would prove fatal. From there, the story goes cold. It's unknown whether Gallagher survived his injury. Otherwise, the house built next door by the English family in 1890 saw the passing of thirty-three-year-old Anna later that year, due to complications from childbirth.

As December 1912 closed, so, too, did the entrance to the Cave of Apparitions. The opening to the Haunted Archway was sealed with dirt that was brought in on a temporary railroad from the site of the old reservoir on Franklin Boulevard and West 38th Street. Today, the entrance to the Cave of Apparitions lies buried under many tons of earth. The cave itself, if it still exists, silently sleeps in a perpetual realm of darkness. Its fairies and ghostly occupants repose in their Plutonian underworld.

Waiting.

Chapter 30

The Wraith on Leading Road

41.45627, -81.71516

Frae ghosties and ghoulies, long-leggettie beasties,
And things that go bump in the night,
Good Lord deliver us.
—A quaint old litany

Just about the time that the Cave of Apparitions on Washington Avenue was being sealed, a new haunting was coming to light near the south end of town. The house in question, 2250 Leading Road, was only five years old at the time of the paranormal report. It was a one-and-a-half-story frame house, painted yellow, that sat on a relatively new road, which fronted a small sweep of old farm and prairie land. By most accounts, the house seemed to give off an unusual air of dreariness. The owners of this domicile were Hungarian immigrants Louis and Suzanna Nagy, who'd purchased the house in 1911.

In September 1912, August and Nettie Schill took up residency in the rented home with their family of nine, including their four children, Nettie's parents, August's brother and a boarder named Viola Lozynska. More than a month passed before the ghostly activity started to present itself.

It was around eight o'clock at night when the family first heard the strange footfalls coming from the upstairs rooms. These were followed by weird cries and shivery moans. Then the doors started to open and close on their own. Afterward, loud knockings and sledgehammer-like blows on the doors were heard to echo throughout the house. The Schills were extremely skeptical of anything supernatural but had to accept what was happening in their home as such. Almost immediately, the family moved their beds downstairs and took to sleeping huddled together in two rooms on the ground floor.

In time, word spread throughout the neighborhood of what was transpiring, and many came to experience the disturbances for themselves or to waylay the ghost theory. Stephen and Elizabeth Mondok, who occupied the house next door, heard a tapping on the floor, followed by the sound of a child wailing. Several men of more-than-average courage volunteered to stay in the haunted rooms, but each changed their mind after being frightened out of their wits. Some, after simply hearing the heavy footfalls above, would venture no further than the first floor.

As the story of the haunting spread, it was learned that the house's previous tenants, the Campfield family, had likewise experienced terrible ghostly activity in the home, which prompted them to move out that September. Mabel and Raymond Campfield witnessed things that Mabel described as being "beyond mortal ken."

Whatever this phantom wraith was, it apparently had the ability to take on whatever form it chose. While the Schill family believed it to be some sort of haunting or poltergeist, Mabel Campfield believed, in her time there, that it was something closer to a werewolf or a large bear. One night, when she was giving her baby a bath, she sent her son Arthur upstairs to get something. A minute later, he came running back downstairs screaming. The boy claimed that something big and black, like the head of a bear, came across the floor toward him and chased him out. Mabel went to investigate and was greeted at the top of the stairs by the hideous black creature. To her, it seemed to be almost entirely composed of a head and shoulders, though she could plainly hear its paws shuffling on the floor like sandpaper. She quickly grabbed her children and fled to the house next door. When her husband came home from work, he found his family waiting for him with the neighbors. Returning to their house, the Campfields found the front door wide open, giving them the impression that whatever was inside had since cleared off.

The Schills also witnessed the same entity on the second floor in mid-November. To them, it appeared as a yellowish vapor, out of which protruded the head, shoulders and front legs of a large black bear. The creature seemed to be dragging the misty cloud with much difficulty behind it. Its tiny eyes sparkled with human intelligence, yet its lips were twisted into a sneer of sinister, inhuman malice!

Nettie Schill's brother, John Svoboda, came to the house to spend the night in the back upstairs bedroom, which seemed to be the ghost's

GHOST HOLDS WAKE
· IN HAUNTED HOUSE

Leading Road Family and Neighbors Terrorized by Moans of "Poltergeist."

MANY HEAR "SPOOK"

Voices and Footfalls Keep August Schill Awake for Week.

A headline announces the haunting of the Schill home on Leading Road. *From the* Cleveland Leader, *1912.*

preferred room, in hopes of catching the spectral being in the act. Ten minutes after entering the bedroom, he came back down screaming. According to Svoboda, he first heard heavy footsteps, followed by a puff of smoke rising up from the floor. Then a black object that resembled a large football rolled over and over toward him, as if it had been kicked at him. The smoke made him gag, and he fled the room in terror. "Never again for a thousand dollars," said Svoboda.

On Christmas Eve, Isabelle Dodd, one of the neighbor's children, was visiting the Schills for the holiday. As they were decorating the Christmas tree, she turned and suddenly let out a scream. Standing on the stairs, clad in white, was the apparition of a baby. Isabelle Dodd fled the house as fast as her feet could carry her.

As it turns out, only one death had occurred in the house since its construction in 1907, that of the Campfields' three-year-old son, Raymond Creighton Campfield, who passed on August 16, 1912. The child's sudden death, according to Mabel Campfield, was just one of several terrible things to have befallen her family while living at that house. On hearing the report of a ghostly child standing on the stairs, she refused to believe that it could be the spirit of her recently deceased babe. She could see no reason why he would ever come back from beyond the grave to bother anyone. And while she didn't like to mention it, she admitted that the hideous black creature she and her son encountered on the second floor of the house returned the night before her child died.

Beyond the incident on Christmas Eve, the ghostly presence in the house, on many occasions, was heard descending the stairs with heavy footfalls and twice was heard moving about the first-floor bedrooms where the family slept.

"It is terrible to hear somebody walking down the stairs and not be able to see them," said August Schill. "Maybe you cannot believe. One night I sat there in that chair. Quickly I felt a chill pass over me and I felt fingers on my left shoulder. A voice said 'Go upstairs. It's time.'"

One night, Nettie Schill's mother heard steps in the room in which she was sleeping. Suddenly, a heavy, coarse and calloused hand came down on her and covered her mouth, almost suffocating the life out of her. A moment later, it vanished as though it were a whiff of steam. She firmly believed the phantom to be masculine in nature but couldn't account for the moans and piteous crying, which seemed to be made by a woman. Not long after the experience, Nettie Schill's parents moved to West 4th Street.

On multiple occasions, the windows all rattled violently at once and a loud pounding was heard on the front door. Grabbing his revolver, August Schill would throw open the door, only to find nobody there. He couldn't even find one track in the snow leading to or away from the house. Most disturbances occurred at eight o'clock at night, close to midnight and again between the hours of four and five o'clock in the morning.

The story broke in the newspapers on December 30, and the haunted house on Leading Road became an overnight sensation. August Schill sought at once to put an end to the matter. He quietly enlisted eight men from the neighborhood to stand vigil in the haunted room the following night. The volunteers were Nettie Schill's brothers John and William Svoboda, Frank Hanecek, James Broderick, John Currier, William O'Brien, Joseph Holan Sr. and Joseph Holan Jr.

When Nettie Schill learned of her husband's plan, she suggested that the physicians who attended to three-year-old Raymond Creighton Campfield when he died in the house also be present. The physicians agreed to this, and Drs. Schneider and Crouch and a drugstore clerk named Reis joined the party. That night, a group of between two and three hundred curiosity seekers descended on Leading Road. Twice, the police had to disperse the crowd.

The disturbances started earlier in the evening with the sounds of something shuffling across the floor upstairs. When that noise stopped, it was replaced by the sound of children's voices shrieking, gradually getting higher and higher in pitch, yet there was no echo to the screams. Then, just as suddenly as they started, the screams stopped. At this, Nettie Schill and her children chose to spend that night with neighbors, leaving the watchers to conduct their work. Of those who were in attendance that night, W.J. Reis believed the sounds were coming from rattling pipes and that the rest of the phenomenon had been imagined, despite the reports by multiple credible witnesses.

The following evening, another vigil was kept at the house. The attendants this time were E.G. Parcell; F. Bures; Mr. and Mrs. Carl Nagy, who were the owner's brother and sister-in-law; and Nettie Schill's father, Jacob Svoboda. As the group assembled downstairs, the sound of whistling and scraping was heard in the room above. The party rushed up the stairs but found the room empty. At this, Nettie Schill seemed to suffer some sort of breakdown. Dr. H.C. Barr was sent for and, when he arrived, found her in a state of hysterics. She was promptly removed from the house and taken to the home of her parents but was later brought to Grace Hospital on West 14th Street.

The following evening, the doctors were to return and join August Schill in keeping vigil in the haunted room but refused to do so. At this, Schill turned to the assistance of a spiritualist. Reverend H.C. Figures of the First Church of the Soul arrived that night and conducted a one-hour séance in the company of August Schill and a reporter from the *Cleveland Leader*. From this, the spiritualist determined that the house was being haunted by three separate entities, these being an elderly man with white hair, a flowing beard and a cane; a woman; and a baby. The man claimed that they'd been causing the disturbances in reaction to their annoyance at the presence of the Schills' boarder, Viola Lozynska, whom they claimed was an unknowing medium.

That was it. August Schill packed up every scrap and shred that he and his family owned and moved out the following night. Within a day or two, Nettie Schill had fully recovered from her breakdown and was settled peacefully into her new home on West 48th Street. She vowed never to return to the house on Leading Road, not even if she were offered $10,000.

Meanwhile, Suzanna Nagy—who, with her husband, Louis, owned the house—arrived at the Leading Road home to take up watch and wait for the ghost to appear. She and her husband, greatly perturbed by the Schills' sudden departure, as well as by the reputation that their property had earned, determined to move into the house themselves and remain there until the cause of the disturbances could be discovered.

The following day, Louis Nagy arrived with a horse-drawn cart containing all their worldly possessions. As the cart stopped in front of the Leading Road house, the horse fell dead! Instantly, the neighbors attributed the animal's sudden demise to whatever it was that lurked within the house. As Suzanna Nagy explained to them that the horse was old and

A view of Leading Avenue today. *Photo by William G. Krejci.*

LOST GHOST STORIES OF CLEVELAND

near the end of its time, her husband unloaded the cart and moved their belongings in. Though they gave no credence to the stories about what had been happening in their house, the Nagys admitted that the room on the second floor where the majority of the disturbances had been reported was not to be inhabited by their family.

A week later, the Nagys claimed that their cat, St. Anthony by name, had gone upstairs into the haunted room and killed something, though no body of any animal could be found. This, they hoped, would finally put to rest the stories of the ghost. Still, the Nagys only lived in the house briefly after the Schills moved out and departed after less than a year. By the middle of 1913, a tailor named Vaclav Csiszar was renting the house.

In 1920, the address of the house was changed from 4250 Leading Road to 4222 Leading Avenue. That year also saw a brief return by the Nagys, who ultimately rid themselves of the property and sold the house in 1921.

No further ghostly activity was reported in the home beyond early 1913. While a small portion of Leading Avenue remains, the south end of the street, including the haunted house, was demolished in the 1950s to make way for the entrance ramp from Fulton Road to the southbound lanes of Interstate 71.

CHAPTER 31

THE GRANGER ROAD PEST HOUSE

BRICK BUILDING: 41.41697, -81.62693
SMALLPOX BUILDING: 41.41802, -81.62705

I dwell in a lonely house I know
That vanished many a summer ago,
And left no trace but the cellar walls,
And a cellar in which the daylight falls
And the purple-stemmed wild raspberries grow.
—"Ghost House" by Robert Frost

By and large, hospitals prior to the twentieth century were anything but places of wellness and recovery. In too many cases, a patient checked in but never checked out—not alive, at least. Medical institutions were breeding grounds of plague and illness, a far cry from the facilities we know today.

Realizing that disease was easily spread among patients, a thought was put forth by medical experts to isolate the most contagious of cases; thus, pesthouses were established. Also referred to as infectious disease hospitals, pesthouses were usually set as far from densely populated areas as possible, so as to avoid sickness from getting out and infecting the general public. It should also be noted that admittance to the pesthouse wasn't voluntary. If it was learned that an individual had contracted a highly transmissible illness, that person would be "collected" and brought to one of these isolated locations, oftentimes to die.

As far as Cleveland is concerned, the most infectious cases were originally housed at the City Infirmary on Scranton Road, which today operates as

Old Granger Road now abruptly ends at a wooded hillside. *Photo by William G. Krejci.*

MetroHealth Medical Center. In 1876, a new pesthouse was opened on present-day Ridge Road at what had formerly been the Silberg Brothers Winery. That facility was in use until 1898, at which time it was closed; in 1900, it reopened as West Park Cemetery. Patients were briefly held again at the City Infirmary but, in 1899, were again moved. The new site chosen was many miles outside of town on a hillside in Independence Township.

The parcel was composed of nearly nine acres of land and was situated above the small, unincorporated village of Willow. This was located near the intersection of present-day East 71st Street and Canal Road. The site was on a promontory about halfway up the east slope of the Cuyahoga River escarpment, where Old Granger Road once made a sharp switchback before completing its climb to the heights above. The site now rests within the boundaries of Garfield Heights.

In the early 1870s, a frame house was built on the lot by Peter Drescher, whose parents briefly resided in nearby Newburgh Township. Ultimately, the entire family moved west to Dover Township and settled in what is now Westlake. When the City of Cleveland purchased the site, it made use of the house that already existed and proceeded to build two more structures.

The first of these was an ornate building referred to as the Brick House, sometimes called the Brick Hospital. A little farther to the northeast of this, an oblong frame structure was erected. This was the Smallpox Building. Also called the Detention House, it was where the worst cases were housed and likely saw the most deaths.

On the south end of the property, closest to the road, was the main office building, called the Red House, owing to the color it was painted. This was the same house that Peter Drescher had built more than twenty-five years earlier.

Curiously, the pesthouse on Granger Road was only temporarily used. In 1901, a new pesthouse was opened on the grounds of the City Infirmary, though both sites remained in operation through the smallpox epidemic of 1902. The following year, the facility on Granger Road was closed and the one at the City Infirmary was converted into a tuberculosis ward. At this, all patients were moved to the new Cooley Farm facility in Warrensville.

In the end, it was determined that the biggest problem with the Granger Road Pest House was its accessibility. The road to reach it was quite steep, considered treacherous at best and extremely difficult to ascend.

After its closing, the buildings on the site fell into disrepair. By 1912, the nine acres of land had devolved into a weed-choked wilderness of tall grass and become a mournful spectacle of decay. Tramps and vagabonds frequently used the Smallpox Building and Brick House as places of refuge from the cold. The wooden steps that led to the ornamental front porch of the Brick House had long since been pulled up and burned by squatters for heat. Doors and window sashes throughout the house met with similar fates, and not a single pane of glass remained. Beds and filthy mattresses were cast about carelessly. Holes were intentionally knocked through every wall, and rain poured in through open transom windows. The nearby Smallpox Building had fallen into an equally deplorable condition. As it saw occasional tenancy, only the Red House was kept in a somewhat livable state.

It was around 1912 that the City of Cleveland looked again at repairing and reopening the hospital on Granger Road, as the one in Warrensville was needed for other purposes. Following an appraisal in February 1913, it was determined that the pesthouse on Granger Road was the least valuable property that Cleveland owned. That October, the city opted instead to lease the property to the nearby Newburgh Brick and Clay Company, which wished to use the buildings as employee housing. The terms were fifteen dollars per month for the next two years.

A problem arose in the fact that former mayor Herman Baehr had appointed William Sisson to the post of custodian of the facility three years earlier. Even though the hospital had been closed since 1903, Sisson resided there with his wife and three daughters and kept the Red House, which they occupied, in relatively decent order. Sisson protested an eviction and was permitted to remain in the house.

The Newburgh Brick and Clay Company's attempt at using the other former pesthouse buildings for employee housing was a complete failure. The workers refused to stay in the buildings, and the company failed to provide proper living quarters. After a short time, the men sought employment and shelter elsewhere. Losing money on the lease agreement, the company rented the Brick House to Alfred and Nina Golden. At that time, Alfred was employed as a farmhand on the Honeywell Farm in nearby Newburgh. Alfred Golden paid the company five dollars a month and took up residency with his wife and child on the derelict property. At this, he started the long process of making the building somewhat habitable.

Of course, it was rumored throughout the area that both the Brick House and Smallpox Building were extremely haunted by white-robed ghosts and hobgoblins of the lowest order. When asked about this, Nina Golden said that, although she'd only been in the house for two weeks, she'd yet to see a ghost of any form. There were also stories of a ghostly woman in a white dress who was reported to awaken the tramps that slept in the buildings, but this woman in white hadn't been seen by the Goldens either.

As the years passed, the tenants moved away, and the buildings on the old pesthouse grounds fell into further disrepair. What vandals and vagrants started, time finished. Visiting the site today can be quite difficult. Old Granger Road abruptly ends at a wooded hillside; from there, the road is completely gone. On a promontory above the dead end rests the site of the

Foundation ruins are all that remain of the Granger Road Pest House. *Photo by William G. Krejci.*

old pesthouse. The Red House and Smallpox Building have both long since vanished. By all appearances, the Brick House seems to have collapsed down the hillside. All that remains are a few foundations where the cellars were once located.

It truly is a desolate spot, that lonesome hillside. It affects the senses, especially when the wind howls up the steep embankment and whips through the briars and the bracken. Can a site such as this still be haunted, so long after its houses have fallen? The isolated locale of the Granger Road Pest House certainly feels as though it must be.

BIBLIOGRAPHY

Ancestry. https://www.ancestry.com.

Atlas of Cuyahoga County and the City of Cleveland, Ohio. Chicago: Geo. F. Cram, 1892.

Atlas of Cuyahoga County Outside Cleveland. Cleveland, OH: Basalt, Hatch & Company, 1903.

Avery, Elroy McKendree. *A History of Cleveland and Its Environs.* Cleveland, OH: Lewis Publishing, 1918.

Basilone-Jones, Ann, and Ashley Moran. *Milan.* Charleston, SC: Arcadia Publishing, 2015.

Becker, Thea Gallo. *Lakewood.* Charleston, SC: Arcadia Publishing, 2003.

Blackmore, Harris H., and Fred Mayer's Lithography. *Map of Cuyahoga County, Ohio.* Cleveland, OH: Stoddard & Everett, 1852.

Brown, James P. *Atlas of the Suburbs of Cleveland, Ohio.* Philadelphia: A.H. Mueller, 1898.

Cincinnati Post. December 2, 1884.

Cincinnati Semi-Weekly Gazette. March 11, 1873.

City Atlas of Cleveland, Ohio: From Official Records, Private Plans and Actual Surveys. Philadelphia: G.M. Hopkins, 1881.

Cleveland Advertiser. 1831–35.

The Cleveland Blue Book. Cleveland, OH: Helen de Kay Townsend, 1935.

Cleveland City Directories. 1837–1915.

Cleveland Daily Advertiser. 1836–38.

Cleveland Daily Herald. 1836–75.

Cleveland Daily Leader. February 15, 1867.

Cleveland Herald. 1843–53.

Cleveland Historical. https://clevelandhistorical.org.

Cleveland Leader. 1854–1913.

Cleveland Memory. http://www.clevelandmemory.org.

Cleveland Press. September 9, 1902.

Cleveland Public Library. https://cpl.org.

Cleveland Register. January 25, 1820.

Cleveland Weekly Advertiser. August 17, 1837.

Cleveland Weekly Plain Dealer. 1854–66.

Columbus Dispatch. August 4, 2002.

Daily People (New York, NY). August 31, 1912.

Democrat Pioneer (Upper Sandusky, OH). January 30, 1846.

Detroit Times. October 24, 1908.

Evening Post (New York, NY). November 15, 1851.

FamilySearch. https://www.familysearch.org/.

Fiege, Father Marianus. *The Princess of Poverty: Saint Clare of Assisi and the Order of Poor Ladies*. Evansville, IN: Poor Clares of the Monastery of S. Clare, 1909.

Find a Grave. https://www.findagrave.com.

Firelands Historical Society. *The Firelands Pioneer*. Norwalk, OH: Firelands Historical Society, 1868.

Flynn, Thomas. *Atlas of the Suburbs of Cleveland, Ohio*. Philadelphia: A.H. Mueller, 1898.

Gehring, Blythe R. *Vignettes of Clifton Park*. Cleveland, OH: Penton Press, 1970.

GenealogyBank. https://www.genealogybank.com/.

Gerstner, Patsy. *The Medical Institutions of Cleveland: 1813–1910*. Cleveland, OH: n.p., 2002.

Gresser, John A. *Burials and Removals Erie Street Cemetery, 1840–1918*. Cleveland, OH: n.p., 1919.

History of Trumbull and Mahoning Counties. Cleveland, OH: H.Z. Williams & Bro., 1882.

Hopkins, Griffith Morgan, Jr., and S.H. Mathews. *Map of Cuyahoga County, Ohio: From Actual Surveys & County Records, Under the Supervision of G.M. Hopkins Jr. C.E.* Philadelphia: S.H. Mathews, 1858.

Insurance Maps of Cleveland, Ohio. Vols. 1–12. New York: Sanborn Map & Publishing, 1886–1918.

Johnson, Crisfield. *History of Cuyahoga County, Ohio: In Three Parts, With Portraits and Biographical Sketches of Its Prominent Men and Pioneers*. Cleveland, OH:

Greater Cleveland Genealogical Society, 1879.

Kennedy, James Harrison. *A History of the City of Cleveland. Its Settlement, Rise and Progress, 1796–1896.* Cleveland, OH: Imperial Press, 1897.

Kennedy, James Harrison, and Wilson Miles Day. *The Bench and Bar of Cleveland.* Cleveland, OH: Cleveland Printing and Publishing, 1889.

Krause, F.L. *Atlas of the City of Cleveland Ohio.* Philadelphia, PA: A.H. Mueller, 1898.

Lake, D.J. *Atlas of Cuyahoga County, Ohio: From Actual Surveys by and under the Directions of D.J. Lake, C.E.* Philadelphia: Titus, Simmons & Titus, 1874.

Library of Congress. https://www.loc.gov.

Maps of Cuyahoga County Outside of Cleveland. Cleveland, OH: H.B. Stranahan, 1903.

Merchant, Ahaz. *Cleveland and Environs.* Cleveland, OH: Ahaz Merchant, 1835.

Monroe Street Cemetery Foundation. https://mscf1841.org.

New York Dispatch. March 4, 1866.

New York Herald. January 15, 1886.

Northern Ohio Journal (Painesville, OH). March 15, 1873.

Orth, Samuel P. *A History of Cleveland Ohio.* Cleveland, OH: S.J. Clark Publishing, 1910.

Payne, William. *Cleveland Illustrated, A Pictorial Hand-Book of the Forest City.* Cleveland, OH: Fairbanks, Benedict, 1876.

Plain Dealer (Cleveland, OH). 1842–1973.

Plat Book of Cuyahoga County, Ohio. Vols. 1–7. Philadelphia: G.M. Hopkins Company, 1920–43.

Plat Book of the City of Cleveland, Ohio and Suburbs, Complete in Two Volumes: From Official Records, Private Plans and Actual Surveys. Philadelphia: G.M. Hopkins Co., 1912–14.

Progressive Men of Northern Ohio. Cleveland, OH: Plain Dealer Publishing, 1906.

Repository (Canton, OH). 1886–1908.

Savannah Morning News. December 3, 1884.

Sisseton (SD) Weekly Standard. November 6, 1908.

Spectator (New York, NY). May 15, 1851.

Stansbury, Howard. *Survey of the Harbor of Cleveland, Ohio.* Cleveland, OH: Capt. Howard Stansbury, 1853.

Stone, Lucy Gallup, and Tamzen E. Haynes. *History of Strongsville, Cuyahoga County, Ohio; with Illustrations.* Berea, OH: Republican Printing, 1901.

Stoner, J.J. *Birds Eye View of Cleveland Ohio 1877.* Madison, WI: J.J. Stoner, 1877.

Taylor, Henry. *General History of Macon County Missouri.* Chicago: Henry

Taylor, 1910.

Topeka State Journal. August 31, 1912.

United States Patenting Office. *Annual Report of the Commissioner of Patents.* Washington, DC: U.S. Government Patenting Office, 1855–56.

Van Tassel, David D., and John J. Grabowski, eds. *The Encyclopedia of Cleveland History.* Bloomington: Indiana University Press, in association with Case Western Reserve University and the Western Reserve Historical Society, 1996.

Vigil, Vicki Blum. *Cemeteries of Northeast Ohio: Stones, Symbols & Stories.* Cleveland, OH: Gray, 2007.

Watkins (NY) Democrat. March 16, 1893.

Western Intelligencer (Cleveland, OH). 1827–28.

Western Reserve Historical Society. https://www.wrhs.org.

West Side Sentinel (Cleveland, OH). May 1880.

Wheeling (WV) Register. November 29, 1884.

Whittlesey, Charles. *Early History of Cleveland with Biographical Notices of the Pioneers and Surveyors.* Cleveland, OH: Higgins, 1867.

Wickham, Gertrude Van Rensselaer. *Pioneer Families of Cleveland, 1796–1840.* Cleveland, OH: Evangelical, 1914.

ABOUT THE AUTHOR

Photo courtesy Christina Johnson.

William G. Krejci was born in Cleveland and raised in neighboring Avon Lake. With an interest in local history, he spends much of his time investigating the origins of ghostly legends and urban lore. He is also the owner and host of Strange & Spooky Cleveland Tours. Since 2022, he has served on the board of the Monroe Street Cemetery Foundation. William is the author of *Buried Beneath Cleveland: Lost Cemeteries of Cuyahoga County*, *Haunted Put-in-Bay*, *Ghosts and Legends of Northern Ohio*, *Lost Put-in-Bay* and the *Jack Sullivan Mysteries* and the coauthor of *Haunted Franklin Castle*. In his free time, he enjoys hiking, playing guitar and singing in an Irish band.

FREE eBOOK OFFER

Scan the QR code below, enter your e-mail address and get our original Haunted America compilation eBook delivered straight to your inbox for free.

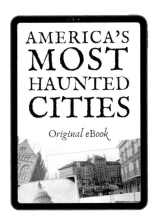

ABOUT THE BOOK

Every city, town, parish, community and school has their own paranormal history. Whether they are spirits caught in the Bardo, ancestors checking on their descendants, restless souls sending a message or simply spectral troublemakers, ghosts have been part of the human tradition from the beginning of time.

In this book, we feature a collection of stories from five of America's most haunted cities: Baltimore, Chicago, Galveston, New Orleans and Washington, D.C.

SCAN TO GET
AMERICA'S MOST HAUNTED CITIES

Having trouble scanning? Go to:
biz.arcadiapublishing.com/americas-most-haunted-cities

Visit us at
www.historypress.com